PRENTICE HALL

Pocket Guide
for Writers

Anthony C. Winkler

JoRay McCuen

Glendale College

PRENTICE HALL, ENGLEWOOD CLIFFS, NJ 07632

Library of Congress Cataloging-in-Publication Data

Winkler, Anthony C.
    The Prentice Hall pocket guide for writers / Anthony Winkler,
JoRay McCuen.
        p.   cm.
    ISBN 0-13-309717-X
    1. English language—Rhetoric—Handbooks, manuals, etc.
I. McCuen, Jo Ray.   II. Title
PE1408.W6195 1995
808' .042—dc20   94-34485
                                                             CIP

Editorial/production supervision: *Maureen Richardson*
Acquisitions editor: *Alison Reeves*
Editor-in-chief: *Anthony English*
Interior/Cover Design: *Gregory Morgan, Diana McKnight at
  Joseph Rattan Design, Dallas*
Manufacturing buyer: *Aloka Rathnam*

© *1995 by Prentice-Hall, Inc.*
A Simon & Schuster Company
Englewood Cliffs, NJ 07632

Printed in the United States of America
10 9 8 7 6 5 4 3 2 1

ISBN 0-13-309717-X

Prentice-Hall International (UK) Limited, London
Prentice-Hall of Australia Pty. Limited, Sydney
Prentice-Hall Canada Inc., Toronto
Prentice-Hall Hispanoamericana, S.A., Mexico
Prentice-Hall of India Private Limited, New Delhi
Prentice-Hall of Japan, Inc., Tokyo
Simon & Schuster Asia Pte. Ltd., Singapore
Editora Prentice-Hall do Brasil, Ltda., Rio de Janeiro

Contents

CHAPTER 3

FIND YOUR PURPOSE, POINT AND POSTURE 39

CHAPTER 4

MAKE YOUR POINT 55

CHAPTER 5

SUPPORT YOUR POINT 76

CHAPTER 6

Preface

The Prentice-Hall Pocket Guide for Writers is intended as a handy overview of the basic principles behind the writing process. We believe that too much theory and too many examples in a text are apt to muddy, rather than clarify, explanation. We therefore cover, as briefly as possible, all the major steps a writer must take to complete a writing project, and we do so with a minimum of explanation and examples.

The steps we cover are dictated as much by practicality and common sense as by theory. They are, in succession: Find Your Topic; Find Your Purpose, Point and Posture: Make Your Point; Support Your Point; and Clarify Your Point, the last chapter being a brief and practical discussion of how to cultivate a working style.

We use the axioms about the writing process as ground-zero for this book. The first is that some writing cannot be taught. Poetry and works of the imagination fall into this category. Our second assumption is that all other writing, especially expository prose, is highly teachable. It is this kind of writing that is the focus of this book.

To teach expository prose, we subdivide it into two major types: personal and objective writing. Over the years we have learned that students tend to misunderstand these two assignments. We have received many essays on personal topics written with an unjustified stiltedness. And we have likewise gotten many objective essays in which the writer has mistakenly overpersonalized the topic. Here we teach the difference between these two essays. We explain what the personal essay requires–a personal voice and documentation from the writer's own observations; and what the objective essay requires–personal opinion that is supported by external citations and facts.

This book is brief on purpose. We think the best expository prose is brief and to the point, and we have tried hard to reflect these virtues in our own style. It is also an unabashedly student-centered book, with most of its examples being drawn from the works of students, and with every chapter ending with brief but practical exercises that reinforce the content covered.

Many people have contributed to this book with wise counsel and helpful suggestions. Among them are Thomas Dean, Cardinal Stritch College; Janice M. Jones, Kent State University; Fredrick C. Van Hartesveldt, III, Grand Rapids Community College; Nancy Cox, Arkansas Technical University; Carole C. Koroma, Grand Rapids Community College; and Audrey J. Roth, Miami-Dade Community College.

Anthony C. Winkler and JoRay McCuen

Writing From Start to Finish

BLANK PAPER ······ Find Your Topic ·····> **YOU HAVE FOUND YOUR TOPIC**

For personal writing:
concentrate, freewrite,
doodle-think

For objective writing:
read books and periodicals
Check with experts

······ Find Your Point ·····

Ask yourself what reaction you want
Have an attitude toward your subject
Write your main idea as one sentence
(thesis)

YOU HAVE FOUND YOUR POINT ······ Develop Your Point ·····> **YOU HAVE DEVELOPED YOUR POINT**

Choose the right strategy,
such as the following:
narration, description, definition,
comparison/contrast,
division/classification, examples,
causal analysis, process

······ Support Your Point ·····

Be exact
Use descriptive details
Cite facts, statistics, authority,
or expert testimony
Use reasoning

YOU HAVE SUPPORTED YOUR POINT ······ Clarify Your Point ·····> **YOU HAVE CLARIFIED YOUR POINT**

Be plain
Be brief
Have polish and flash

Teachable and Unteachable Writing

Let us begin by frankly admitting that some writing cannot be taught. It is a gift from the muse, the genes, God. As an example of writing we think unteachable, consider this paragraph from a letter penned by a Civil War soldier to his wife on the eve of the battle in which he was killed.

> *But, O Sarah! if the dead can come back to this earth and flit unseen around those they loved, I shall always be near you; in the gladdest days and in the darkest nights ... always, always, and if there be a soft breeze upon your cheek, it shall be my breath, as the cool air fans your throbbing temple, it shall be my spirit passing by. Sarah do not mourn me dead; think I am gone and wait for thee, for we shall meet again.*

This kind of extraordinary writing bubbles up like molten lava from some seismic chamber of the heart. It is often spontaneous but seldom controllable, erupting during moments of inspiration, passion, or personal peril. No one knows how to re-create the conditions necessary to produce such writing. It cannot be taught; it can only be learned.

Instead, the kind of writing this book intends to teach is the practical nuts-and-bolts writing of everyday communication. It typically consists of essays, memos, articles, reports, instructions, and notes. It includes any communication based not on imagination but on fact. To dash off a memo or pen a competent essay or article you do not have to be on the eve of battle or lie prostrate on your deathbed. Expository prose, which is the generic name given to factual writing, can be learned by virtually everyone who is willing to work hard.

EXPOSITORY PROSE

Expository prose is the workhorse of textual communication. It is utility prose written to voice an opinion, viewpoint, or fact. Its aim is not the expression of sentiment or feeling, but simple clarity. Done well, it is specific and straightforward, says something definite, and uses words efficiently to make a point; done poorly, its sentences are pulpy and vague, and its opinions seem to flip-flop about on the page like a hooked fish. Good expository prose uses figurative language not for its own sake, but to further highlight a point.

Here is an example of flawed expository prose.

It has come to our attention that an elderly female, whose place of residence is a leather foot covering, has dependents who are so numerous that she fails to comprehend the proper course of action she should pursue.

— Gayle White, "Ever Wonder Why You're in a Fog?"
Atlanta Constitution, *October 10, 1978*

This is flawed expository prose because the writer's meaning is muddied up by wordiness. What this writer really meant to say was, "There was an old woman who lived in a shoe. She had so many children, she didn't know what to do."

Conversely, here is an example of good expository prose.

It is widely believed that every word has a correct meaning, that we learn these meanings principally from teachers and grammarians (except that most of the time we don't bother to, so that we ordinarily speak "sloppy English"), and that dictionaries and grammars are the supreme authority in matters of meaning and usage. Few people ask by what authority the writers of dictionaries and grammars say what they say. I once got into a dispute with an English woman over the pronunciation of a word and offered to look it up in the dictionary. The English woman said firmly, "What for? I am English. I was born and brought up in England. The way I speak is English." Such self-assurance about one's language is not uncommon among the English. In the United States, however, anyone who is willing to quarrel with the dictionary is regarded as either eccentric or mad.

—*S. I. Hayakawa, "How Dictionaries Are Made"*

This is good expository prose because the writer has a point, makes it, backs it up, and does so in a style that combines briskness with clarity.

Unless you are a hermit marooned on an island with no one to mutter to but a dog-eared diary, sooner or later you will have to try your hand at expository writing. You will write it at work in memos, letters, and reports; at school in essays; and at home in notes to your landlord about a leaky faucet or missiles to your neighbor about her pesky dog. Such expository writing, done well, will invariably embody four basic principles: have a point, state the point, prove the point, and clarify the point.

To teach you how to practice these principles in your writing is the ambition of this book.

COLLEGE WRITING AND THE REAL WORLD

Essay writing is not some academic gruel fiendishly cooked up by sadistic English teachers, as some of our students have been heard to mutter darkly. If anything, the classroom accurately reflects the editorial conditions under which professional writers often work.

For example, students write for an admittedly hodgepodge audience—an instructor, their classmates, or an imagined group of readers at whom they may have been directed to slant an essay. We have heard students carp that this arrangement is an artifice of the classroom. But it is not. Unless they are self-published, professional writers scribble for exactly the same hodgepodge: they write for an editor, for their peers, and for the eventual readership at whom the work is aimed.

Students are often given broad, open-ended assignments, such as "write about any process with which you are familiar," and many have wailed within our earshot about such vagueness. The professional is likewise only rarely told how to slant an article or essay. More likely the assignment will be a spongy editorial order to write a story about so-and-so, with the emphasis and approach being left entirely to the writer.

Finally, students must often labor over topics they think hideous, the most infamous example being, "write an essay about how you spent your last summer vacation." The few lucky exceptions aside, all professional writers who write *only* about beloved topics are dead—of starvation. When they get to heaven, professional writers will, it is hoped, get to write solely about topics that please them. But on this earthly plane they must toil daily over topics they regard as wretched, routine, and humdrum.

Classroom writing matters. Writing essays is excellent practice for all kinds of expository prose, the pressures and conditions in this class being nearly identical to those under which you will later work.

SOME GENERAL OBSERVATIONS ABOUT WRITING

Writing methods vary dramatically both with the writer and the assignment. Some writers, after a brief period of incubation, hemorrhage words onto the page. Others drip like leaky faucets in the dark night. Some plot out ahead of time every paragraph they intend to write. Others hatch their ideas spontaneously in a dungeon of the subconscious and awake scribbling whole sentences.

Indeed, writing is a bit like duck shooting. Some days you will bring down the duck with one clean shot. Other days, you will blast away like a berserk machine gunner and bag only a single bedraggled sentence. All the writing practice in the world cannot guarantee that on any one sitting the words will magically flow and that you will be able to say exactly what you mean.

No book, no principle, no amount of practice can teach a writer how to turn out perfect copy with every try. When it gets better, writing gets better gradually, not suddenly. Dead prose does not rise up from the grave like Lazarus and suddenly sing. If anything, it recovers as a patient does from hoarseness—slowly, and by degrees.

Writing is also hard work, even for the gifted. The idea that the true writer is some blessed soul who can dash off perfect pages at one sitting is a myth. For most writers, writing means slogging through repeated rewrites. "My pencils outlast their erasers," wrote Vladimir Nabokov, the renowned author admired for his beautiful prose style.

Writing typically consists of endless revisions and begets many torn up pages. If you find yourself struggling to get words down on paper and feeling wretchedly frustrated as you do, accept our heartfelt congratulations. You are working exactly like professional writers, who must wrestle daily with the same exasperating ups and downs of their craft.

STEPS YOU CAN TAKE TO MAKE YOURSELF A BETTER WRITER

If you wish to write better expository prose, begin now by taking these practical steps.

❶ When you get an assignment, start working on it right away. Do not dilly-dally or put it off. Never wait to begin until the night before the work is due. Writing anything involves a kind of mental hatching. Start early enough, and give your brain a chance to hatch ideas about the assignment. Otherwise, it will hatch an egg.

❷ Look up the facts. Most expository prose consists not of generalizations but facts. If you think you can fake facts, you are mistaken. Start reading early on the topic. Taking in facts about it will help form your opinion and start the process of mental hatching.

❸ Write at least three drafts. The first draft should be a no-holds-barred attempt to get something down on paper. The second draft is where you tidy up your ideas, straighten out your sentences, shift paragraphs, or add clarifications. The third is where you dust for bad grammar, wipe up clutter, and polish the punctuation. Write fewer than three drafts, and you are likely to be disappointed at the outcome.

Remember that the best writing occurs by accretion—the same process used by the oyster to make a pearl. It is a laborious search over a period for the right theme, note, idea, or word. The process consists of repeated tinkering, revision, and rethinking of the subject. Here, for example, is a newspaper description of how Dr. Martin Luther King, Jr., worked on his famous "I Have a Dream" speech.

He worked through the night on the eve of the march, occasionally raising his head and asking, "Can you give me another word for. . . ?"

But Martin Luther King Jr.'s historic speech was not a last-minute affair. Coretta Scott King remembers her husband talking about the ideas it contained in the days leading up to the march. Looking back, she reflects that he might have been juggling the needs to both inspire and inform, to present both substance and vision.

—*"The Birth of a Speech,"* Atlanta Constitution,
August 21, 1983

This is how veteran writers really work. To become the best writer you can be, you must acquire similar work habits.

EXERCISES

❶ From a magazine or book, excerpt a paragraph you consider excellent writing. Write down the reasons you consider it so.

❷ Make a list of the kinds of expository prose you had to write within the last month. State which of these assignments was easiest and which the most difficult. Offer reasons for your judgment.

❸ Write a paragraph describing the ideal place to live, making three drafts according to rule 3 on p. 8. Compare your third draft with the first.

Find Your Topic

Writing is thinking. If you write poorly, it is possible that your style is flawed, your grammar incorrect, or your topic ill chosen. But it is far more likely that your thinking was faulty. Through practically all good expository writing runs careful thinking that is visible in the language, details, and logical flow of a paper. Write poorly, and your thinking—not your tennis elbow—will justly take the rap.

Writing invariably involves thinking through and making a series of progressively narrow choices. You choose a topic from a subject. From the topic, you choose a certain point as your theme. To express this point, you choose a particular posture or emphasis and an overall purpose for your essay. When the time comes to actually write, you choose to garb your ideas in certain words and sentence patterns and to support them with particular details.

Even if you do not consciously make these choices—if you do not say aloud, "this statement will be my main point, this idea my purpose, and this concept my posture"—you still implicitly make them. To write one sentence is to have chosen it over another. To use one word is to have rejected a score of others. To imprint your thoughts over the vast tundra of the empty page, you must make these choices.

Sometimes all the thinking and choosing are done during the fumbling of writing. This chapter, for example, was begun in one form and ended up as another. It has had at least three past lives during which it was once fatter, then thinner, until it reached its present heft. Each version evolved from the actual writing as we struggled to say what we thought we meant to say. That is one way to work.

But it is not the way we recommend for the beginner. What we recommend, instead, is thinking about your writing choices and making them more or less deliberately.

Let us start from scratch. You have been given a writing assignment, and it requires you to logically narrow a broad subject into a specific topic. Many college assignments are deliberately worded to be such an exercise in thinking. A few assignments, such as "contrast an uncle with an aunt," will need no further narrowing. But far more typical is the broadly worded assignment, such as this one: "Write an essay about an important institution." What do you do first?

First, you narrow the subject into a suitable topic.

SUBJECT AND TOPIC

The subject is the broad area mapped out by the wording of the assignment; the topic is a logical part of the subject, what a mathematician might call its subset. In the assignment, "write an essay about an important institution," "important institution" is the subject. If you wrote about the specific institution of marriage, that would be your topic.

Subject and topic share the blood lines that exist between the whole and the part. If your subject is "an important institution," your topic cannot be "your favorite vacation spot." Likewise, if your subject is to write about "an intimidating person," your topic cannot be "marriage." "Marriage" is not a logical subset of "an intimidating person"; "favorite vacation spot" is not part of "an important institution."

Some other examples of actual subjects and the logical topics student writers whittled from them are shown on page 14.

The next step is to decide whether the assignment requires personal or impersonal writing.

SUBJECT	TOPIC
Write an essay on a theory in sonality psychology.	Four basic human per-types
Write about a social problem.	Child molestation
Define a common term or phrase.	Sibling rivalry
Write about an event that changed your life.	Death of my grand-mother
Compare and contrast two famous historical events.	The murdur of Julius Caesar and Czar Nicholas II.
The causes of poverty.	Economic depression, mental illness, and cultural prejudices as roots of poverty in the U.S.

KINDS OF WRITING ASSIGNMENTS: OBJECTIVE AND PERSONAL

Objective writing, as the name implies, is writing that focuses more on the topic and less on the individuality of the writer. It requires objective research and a detached weighing of facts and opinions. The working viewpoint in such a paper is that of the unbiased researcher, "I" being banned as unscholarly. Personal writing, on the other hand, specifically asks for a writer's own experiences and observations, and demands the use of "I." You must say what you personally think and can revel in your projected personality.

Here are some examples of objective and personal writing assignments.

OBJECTIVE WRITING ASSIGNMENTS

❶ Write an essay defining prejudice.

❷ Write an essay tracing the roots of urban poverty.

❸ Discuss one of Plato's major contributions to Western thought.

❹ Contrast the styles of two twentieth-century painters.

❺ Attack or defend the jury system.

PERSONAL WRITING ASSIGNMENTS

❶ Write an essay about a tender moment in your life.

❷ Describe your room as a reflection of yourself.

❸ Write an essay describing your method of studying.

❹ Analyze the role of romance in your human relationships.

❺ Write an essay about an event that changed your life.

Making the distinction between personal and objective writing will tell you exactly where to look for your topic. You will find the topic of the personal writing assignment only by peering deep inside your own self. To find the topic of an objective writing assignment, however, you must search external sources—books, journals, magazines, and experts.

FINDING THE TOPIC OF A PERSONAL WRITING ASSIGNMENT

Let us assume that you have to write a personal essay about the most intimidating person you have ever met. How do you go about narrowing this subject to the topic of a particular person?

Concentrate   Sit in a quiet corner, and think with a notebook in hand. Jot down what you remember most about this frightening person. Scribble down shuddering descriptions of how he or she made you feel. Give yourself time to incubate the subject. Soon debris from your sunken memory will come bubbling to the surface providing you both with a topic as well as the raw material for your personal essay.

Freewrite   The procedure for freewriting is simple. You sit down and write. You do not hesitate or ponder; you simply keep the pen moving or the keyboard clicking. If you find yourself wavering, write down a filler sentence, such as "I can't think," repeatedly until you can think of something else. Abandon all pretense of editorial control. The idea is to undam memory and splatter the page with your raw, unfiltered feelings about the subject.

Here is an example of freewriting on the subject of an "intimidating person."

Intimidating person. Intimidating
person. Who was an intimidating person? Mother Antininous, the nun who
taught me English in junior high. I
can hear her screaching now over the
Palmer method. Then there was Mr.
MacFarland who loved to beat us with
his cane. I hated both of them. I
can't think. I can't think. Well, you
better think, for you have an essay
to write. Then there was this boy in
Junior College who used to snarl at
me whenever we met in public over
some imagined offence. I never found
out what he had against me. I can't
think. I can't think. My father used
to be intimedating but now that he's
dead he doesn't seem so scary, and
now that I'm older his memory is more
irksome than frightening, for there
were a lot of little nonsensical
things that would set him off into a
rage. I can't think. Who was the
worst? Mother Antininous with her
stories about how we'd go to hell if
we split infinitives or dangled par-
ticipals and how as we burned and
wallowed in the fire we shriek with

> regret that we hadn't taken pains to
> learn God's grammar. She was not only
> intimidating, she was a nasty old
> woman who smelled bad and had the
> stench of brimstone all over her
> nun's black robe.

Notice that bobbing in this torrential flood are misspelled words as well as shards of cracked grammar. That is exactly the kind of gushing freewriting should produce. It should not be disciplined or controlled, but merely honest.

After the first spate of freewriting, comb through the debris for a topic or theme. For example, the writer of the preceding essay zoomed in on Mother Antininous as his topic. He freewrote further on her, recalling instances and details of her intimidating presence for use in his essay.

Doodle-Think   To doodle-think you need only pad, pencil, and time to think. Write down the broad subject at the top of the page. Below, write the headings "Who," "What," "Where," "When," and "Why." Scribble down any thought about the subject that occurs to you under these headings. When you cannot think, doodle. If you are thinking about a vacation spot and are temporarily stuck, doodle some appealing scene of it. The object is to think creatively about the subject as you try to extract from it an appropriate topic.

Here are examples of doodle-thinking about favorite vacation spots.

Who   Who do I enjoy spending vacations with? Who usually goes with me? On family vacations my brother tends to make me mad and ruin the vacation with his brattiness.

What   What I like to do on vacation is lie on the beach. I like to read. I like to have time to do nothing. I like having no television. I like long cool nights and hot days.

When   I prefer to vacation during the winter when everything is cold in North America and the outside world seems uninhabitable because of the ice and snow. I hate cold weather.

Where   Silver Sands is my favorite vacation spot. I like it because it's in the Jamaican countryside, quiet, uncrowded, and has a nice beach. I like taking walks on the winding roads that twist through the compound and overlook the ocean.

Why   We need to vacation every year to recharge our batteries and get away from the usual boring routine. We go to Jamaica because my Dad discovered Silver Sands by accident when he was in the service and fell in love with it.

Doodle-thinking is more controlled scribbling than freewriting, but just as exempt from the rigidity of syntax and grammar. The aim is to leave a trail of random thinking on the subject out of which you might later sift a topic. Doodling keeps the mind creatively engaged when you draw a blank.

FINDING THE TOPIC OF AN OBJECTIVE WRITING ASSIGNMENT

The general rule of finding a topic for the objective writing assignment is this: write about what you know. A secondary rule is: know about what you write. For the personal writing assignment you can draw on memory, imagination, and personal observation. But objective assignments demand the details of cold, hard facts found in books, magazines, and databases. You must seek out these details even before you begin narrowing the topic.

Here are suggestions on how to systematically search for details and information about your subject.

Find the Key Word in the Assignment   The key word is the most important word (or words) in the assignment. For example, if you are asked to write an essay about an institution, the obvious key word, "institution," must shape the focus of your topic.

Define the Key Word or Words   Once you have isolated the key word, look up its meaning in a general dictionary or encyclopedia. For instance, the term "institution" is defined as "a behavioral pattern important in the life of a society." Find out what particular academic discipline the key word falls under; then look it up in one of the specialized dictionaries of that field. Because "institution" is a widely used concept in sociology, you can consult the *Encyclopedia of Sociology* or the *Handbook of Sociology* for a discussion of its meaning.

Search the Periodical Sources   Most libraries have on-line databases that can give an instant readout of articles in the periodical literature on virtually any subject. Many of these databases cover the *Reader's Guide to Periodical Literature,* the *Humanities Index,* the *Social Sciences Index,* and the *Periodical Abstracts,* the last covering scholarly and general titles. For example, a scan of the *Social Sciences Index* for the word "institution" uncovered 132 articles. You cannot read that many articles, but you can browse the titles for a possible topic.

Narrow the Term   Once you know the meaning of key word or words in the assignment, you can and must logically narrow it. "Institution" is too elephantine to be pinned onto a small essay. What you need to do is choose a specific institution, such as marriage. Then sit at your library's on-line computer, and type in the word "marriage" as a subject request. We did this and were engulfed by a tide of listings ranging from "interracial marriage" to "marriage and Roman law"—both possible topics.

Scan the Library's Book Collection   Circulate among and scan the stacks of books that bear on your possible topic. For instance, if your specific choice of an institution is marriage, the table of contents of books will yield a wealth of topics, such as "homosexual marriages," "polygamous marriages," and "open marriage."

Ask Experts for Suggestions   Experts not only know more about a subject than you do, but they also know where to find the raw materials you can later use to develop your essay. So, if the writing assignment is in sociology, talk to a sociologist about it; to a political science teacher if it is in politics; and to an art teacher or artists if it is in the arts.

Remember, if you are working on a personal assignment and are poring through library books, you are looking for your topic in all the wrong places. On the other hand, if you are doing an impersonal writing assignment, you should definitely get to a library.

Here is a recap of the sequence of steps you can take to narrow a broad subject into a suitable topic.

❶ Classify the assignment either as requiring personal or objective writing.

❷ Read the wording of the assignment and decide whether it needs narrowing.

❸ If you must narrow the subject, identify its key words and look up their meanings.

❹ If it is a personal writing assignment, search your memory and experiences for an appropriate topic.

❺ If it is an objective writing assignment, start reading, talking, and thinking.

❻ Think. Think. Think.

Once you find your topic, you are on your way to assembling the basic elements of your essay. Next, you must conceive of a purpose for your essay, find your main point, and assume a posture for writing it.

EXERCISES

❶ Narrow the following assignments into acceptable topics:

    a. Write about population control.
    b. Write about kinds of religious worship.
    c. Write about the refugee problem.
    d. Write about a recent revolution.

❷ Doodle-think about one of the following topics:

    a. An influential person in my life
    b. Types of friends to whom I am drawn
    c. Role of art in my life
    d. How money affects me

❸ Decide which kind of assignment, personal or objective, best suits the following topics:

    a. Sterilization as a means of population control
    b. Contribution of Walter Phillip Reuther to U.S. automobile workers
    c. Bad habits that inhibit my academic progress
    d. Teapot Dome Scandal and its key players
    e. Scandal that affected my social standing in the community

f. Frederic Chopin and the expression of romanticism

g. My response to romantic music

h. Difficult lessons I have had to learn

❹ List a minimum of three specific sources you could use in writing on one of the following topics:

a. Economy of Haiti

b. Abraham Lincoln and the Mexican War of 1846

c. Smoking and teenagers

d. Invention of the steam engine

e. Problems faced by Islamic women

Sample Objective Essay
Thoughts on Student Leadership
in the Nineties
Michael J. Smith

"Impatient," "extreme," and even "radical" were labels hurled at the aggressive student leaders of the 60s. But the mood has changed. At most public colleges today—unlike the radical but potent '60s—student leadership is passive, benign, and ineffective. Students allow the administration to ignore them and betray their educational rights as they idly stand by. However, a few student bodies are no longer sitting back and taking administrative abuse or neglect. Instead, they have begun fighting back and laying strategic plans to assert their rights. They are contributing their share to educational reform in this country.

An example of this new revolution occurred in one small community college nestled in a suburb of Los Angeles. There, under the pressing leadership of an involved student body president, the students fought back, wrested control of their own budget (which had been used largely for "special projects" of the administration), and agitated until the administration gave them a voice. The students refused to let the administration tell them how to run their government, refused to let the Board of Trustees treat them with patronizing contempt, and refused to let a few student leaders run the student government as if it were a high school social club. These student leaders sacrificed study time to organize protests, to engage the local press to pay attention to their com-

plaints about crucial classes being
cut, higher fees being assessed,
and student services being truncat-
ed—all while teacher and adminis-
trator salaries as well as benefits
were being raised.

The political style of these students was not always agreeable,
refined, or polite. They soon understood the reality that temperament
and style of negotiation must sometimes be adjusted to fit the specific situation. They were reminded
that negotiations cannot always pro-
ceed smoothly when all sides are in
fiery pursuit of contradictory
goals. Even a dignified and elevated
group like the U.S. Supreme Court
admits to having tense meetings. In
fact, in 1994, when U.S. Supreme
Court Justice Blackmun resigned, the
press asked him if he had enjoyed
his tenure on the Supreme Court. And
he replied, "No . . . most of the
time it was very tense . . . and con-
tentious between the justices." In
other words, combative arguments can
prevail even in the most civilized
of arenas. Progress is often controversial, and justice does not always
flow freely or easily.

The bureaucrats at the college mentioned kept insisting that the students should wait patiently for resolutions to their urgent problems. They should wait patiently for the records of the student association's own finances to be released to the students for the first time in forty years. They should wait patiently while the administration made its own interpretation as to whether or not most fees charged to the students were legal. Again, they should wait patiently for additional English and chemistry classes, for tutors during final exams, for replacement of the students' broken-down copy machines, for extended library hours, for the return of a study abroad program, and for saving a stately old oak tree builders threatened to cut down. The Vice President of Student Services kept promising action "some time soon, but not today." Well, patience is fine for campus administrators and faculty leaders who are tenured and have secured jobs. However, patience is seldom a choice for students given limited time in which to make desperately needed changes. If stu-

dent leaders want visible progress,
they must be determined and, if necessary, cast patience to the wind.
If they remain passive, the bureau-
cratic machinery will stall until
those particular activist students
have transferred on.

Most of the criticism heaped on
aggressive student leaders comes
from people who draw their authority
from the very bureaucracy whose
power the student leaders challenge.
Few administrators, for instance,
will risk their reputations as
consensus-seeking team players to
stand behind what their colleagues
consider radical student agitators.
Ironically, sometimes the bitterest
attacks come from students who bene-
fit in some private way from cater-
ing to this bureaucracy. These com-
plainers are easily identified—grov-
eling Uriah Heeps and sniveling
bootlickers who would sell out their
classmates for scholarships, faculty
kudos, or some ceremonial job at
graduation. Even those for whom
leaders negotiate do not always
stand behind the negotiator. History
teaches that as Thomas Jefferson and
George Washington fought to liberate

the colonies from the British crown,
only a minority of the colonists
favored secession. Similarly, student leaders may find themselves in
the college president's office argu-
ing for better student conditions,
alone and forsaken by fellow
students.

This brings to mind the fable of a
little bird freezing in a cow pas-
ture. All of a sudden one of the
hoosiers laid a big warm "prairie
patty" on the bird's head. Safe and
warm, the bird sat content. But
after a while the dung dried up, and
the bird was trapped. Unable to
escape its bondage, it began chirp-
ing madly. Soon a coyote, attracted
by the bird's cries, skulked into
sight, dug the bird out, and—prompt-
ly devoured it. The moral of the
tale can be seen from different
points of view. Bureaucrats would
say that if you are safe and warm in
your little mound of manure, keep
your mouth shut. They would pontifi-
cate that the bird was betrayed by
its own beak. On the other hand,
activists would insist that the
little creature was never powerless
and was devoured because it was

satisfied to sit in the manure so
long that, once it was dug out by
the fox, it no longer knew how to
use its wings, the tools of its
liberation.

Lord Acton said two centuries ago,
"Power corrupts." Well, powerlessness
also corrupts. And lack of power has
truly been the affliction of the student in the 90s. Students who think
they are going to learn anything
about real leadership by following
the rules of the status quo should
learn a lesson from Martin Luther
King, Jr., accused of extremism by
many blacks as well as whites who
hated his march toward justice. Dr.
King said this about extremism: "Was
not Paul an extremist for the
Christian Gospel? Was not the prophet
Amos an extremist for justice?" Dr.
King's only caveat to extremists was,
"Will we be extremists for the
preservation of injustice or the extension of justice?" The goal of student leaders should be to challenge
anyone—administration, faculty, or
students—who stand in the way of the
extension of justice on campus and to
do so by any means necessary, even
extreme ones.

Sample Personal Essay
Buddies
Terry Wilson

Daddy and I were more buddies than father and son. I don't recall a time when he was sober. With every memory I picture him drunk. When I say "drunk," I mean all the way. He would get so bad that he couldn't talk and just made these grunting sounds no one could understand. I knew he was at his limit when he would look at me with his right eye closed so he wouldn't see double just before he was ready to pass out.

He would say, "Toodle, have you got us?" He always called me that when he was loaded.

I'd say, "Yeah, Daddy, I got us."

"Are you sure?"

"Yeah, Daddy."

"All right," he'd always say in a sort of "I'm counting on you" way.

Daddy's face was covered with lines and wrinkles from all those years of drinking, making him look older than he really was. His eyes, if you could see them before he drank too much, were deep blue, like the color an artist paints the sky in a mountain scene. I guess they told more about him than anything else, because if you could catch his glance for a second, you would see a hint of loneliness or maybe some untold sorrow.

I started driving when I was about eight or nine years old. A puny kid, unable to reach the pedals, I would have to sit in Daddy's lap and let him step on the gas or hit the brakes. My legs did grow some after a few years, so eventually I graduated from Daddy's lap to a pillow because I still couldn't see over the steering wheel. A pillow would place me high enough to see through that little arc between the dash and the top of the steering wheel.

We lived up in Amite County, Mississippi, a dry county. The closest place to buy alcohol was a store across the state line. Whenever I stayed with Daddy, we would go there to get a case of Schlitz beer and a fifth of Seagram's V.O. whiskey. Then I would drive us back to my grandma's and we—or most of the time I—would sneak the liquor into the house.

I guess you could say that Daddy was a "closet drunk." Since no alco-

hol was allowed in Grandma's house,
Daddy and I would sneak it in and
hide it in the closet of Daddy's
room. Of course, Grandma knew Daddy
had alcohol in his room, and Daddy
knew that she knew, but neither
would let on to the other.

I'll never forget Daddy's room. He
smoked Pall Mall unfiltered cigarettes, and when you opened the door
to his room, the smell rushed out to
greet you. It had settled into the
curtains, the bed covers, and even
the walls. Then there was the smell
of stale beer. Every so often we
would wait until Grandma left the
house; then we would rush out to
load the trunk of Daddy's car with
empty beer cans and whiskey bottles
that had piled up in his closet.

Daddy and I used to go to
Kentwood, Louisiana, for the week-
end. A roller skating rink and a
theater were there, which I liked to
use. I would drive us to town and I
would skate one night then attend a
movie the next night. Daddy would
drop me off and pick me up when the
movie was over. Usually he would be
so drunk that I couldn't understand
how he had made it; I would just

thank God when I saw the car.

One night, as we were driving home, we passed a cop car. I guess the cop knew something wasn't right when he saw my little head barely even with the steering wheel. In any case, he turned on his lights and came after us. I had felt nervous when we passed him, but when I saw his lights come on, I panicked. I started hollering, or rather begging, Daddy to wake up. He was slumped over against the door, not comprehending what was going on. Since the country lane had no shoulder, I pulled over as close to the ditch as I dared, and the cop pulled in behind us. He got out of his car, walked up to my window, and looked in at me.

"Let me see your license, son," he order in an "I've-got-your-ass-now-boy" tone.

"I don't have any," I whimpered, thankful that I managed at least to get that out. I was picturing myself as a little David looking way up at a giant Goliath. The cop stooped over and looked at Daddy.

"Sir, would you step out of the car, please."

Daddy was looking round, but I don't think he comprehended what was going on yet.

"Daddy, get out. Come on, get out!" I was talking sort of urgent like, and he finally understood. He opened the door and, with effort, managed to get both feet out and on the ground. He grabbed the door and tried to pull himself up, but his legs just didn't seem to want to hold him. He left the car and fell into the ditch—all in one motion. I really felt sorry for him, but it was at the same time funny, too. This cop was standing there seeing everything, so I zipped across the seat and jumped out to help Daddy. Finally, the cop and I managed to raise him off the ground, and the cop took Daddy to jail after first radioing another car to come and drive me home. Grandma was shocked when she saw a police car drive up with me in it. When I told her what had happened, she started crying hysterically.

Daddy was really good-hearted. Every now and then he would show up at the theater or skating rink to pick me up, and he would have some

other old drunk with him who had
laid a sob story on him about how he
hadn't eaten for days. We would then
have to go somewhere to buy that man
food—and Daddy would give him ten or
twenty dollars. I think that made
Daddy feel good, but it aggravated
the hell out of me how he would let
some bum take advantage of his gen-
erous nature.

Almost every time we got back to
Grandma's, Daddy would be so plas-
tered, he could hardly walk. I had
to go around and help him get out of
his car. He would stand up and rock
back and forth, as if ready to go
down any second. I would put his
left arm on my shoulder and hold his
left hand with mine so his arm would
stay around me. Then I would put my
right arm around the lower part of
his back, and we would take off for
the house. I know we must have
looked funny making this winding
trail to the front door. I always
tried to be as quiet as possible so
Grandma wouldn't get up and see that
Daddy was drunk. Finally, making it
to his room, Daddy would just flop
on his bed. I would undress him,
turn him straight, and put his head

on the pillow. Then I would undress, turn out the light, and get into bed, too.

"You got us, Toodle?"

"Yeah, Daddy, I got us."

"I love you, Toodle."

"I love you, too, Daddy."

Find Your Purpose,
Point and Posture

Expository prose usually has a distinct purpose; makes a specific point and, unless it is wishy-washy, commits its writer to a particular posture. When you write expository prose, you have behind you the momentum of purpose; you have ahead of you a reader who expects you to make a point. If the diarist is a duck paddling playfully in a pond, the expository writer is a ship sailing for some definite port to deliver a particular cargo of meaning.

FIND YOUR PURPOSE

After you have found your narrowed topic, you should think next of some clear purpose for your essay. This purpose should be the effect you hope to achieve—how you want your reader to react. Merely to pass the course cannot be your working purpose, as some of our students occasionally argue. Such a purpose is too remote to guide your hand in writing the essay. And what you are after by formulating a purpose for your essay is a guide to the many choices you will have to make in writing it.

In the classroom, it is common to think of

essays as having one of three definite purposes: to explain or inform; to amuse or entertain; to persuade or convince. These categories are admittedly squishy enough to accommodate almost every kind of writing, from formal biblical criticism to an anguished suicide note. But they do provide a writer with helpful limits.

For example, the purpose of an essay about how the U.S. Federal Reserve works is to explain. An essay about slips of the tongue made by elementary students will entertain. An essay encouraging fellow students to do volunteer work will try to convince. Choosing a purpose helps you narrow the choices of diction, syntax, and details. To explain a serious topic, for example, you know not to pile on the zippy one-liners. Likewise, you know that the essay whose purpose is to amuse should not put on a too solemn face. Choosing a purpose will not only guide you in what to write but also in what *not to write*.

An essay begun without a definite sense of purpose will often flounder from the very outset. Here is an example.

```
Hundreds of commuters have to drive
their cars from outlying neighbor-
hoods to the city every weekday.
Speeding along at 70 mph is quite the
```

fashion on the interstates—even with
the speed limit being 55 mph. Playing
dodge the car can be quite a sport
when you have to change lanes. Your
choices include squeezing between
cars rapidly moving along, risking
damage to your car as well as bodily
injury, or painfully waiting for a
slow moving semi to inch along, giving you free passage to change lanes.
Beat the clock is a game that can
really get your heart pumping.

It is difficult to say why this opening paragraph seems so aimless, but after talking to the
student, we blamed its aimlessness on her con-
fessed lack of purpose. She admitted that she
had simply begun to write on the assignment:
"write an essay on some current transportation
problem." She herself had no transportation
problems. She had noticed that rush-hour
snarls were particularly hideous in the morn-
ings, and she thought to take a stab at this topic
and see what happened. Nothing happened;
she simply went round and round about clot-
ted traffic and surly drivers in the same vein as
her opening paragraph.

After some editorial discussion and a round
of freewriting to further explore her feelings
about the topic, she decided to write an essay

whose purpose would be to convince the reader of the need for mass transit in large cities. She did the necessary digging for facts and details, roughed out a frame of the essay, and began the writing. The opening paragraph of her second try follows:

> An indisputable fact of transportation is that automobile manufacturers will always be able to build cars faster than civil engineers can build the roads to accommodate them. Take, for example, North Atlanta, where after some twenty years of bickering and ten years of acquiring the necessary right of way, the Georgia 400 highway was driven like a concrete spear through the heart of one of Atlanta's oldest and prettiest neighborhoods, forcing families out of their homes and destroying yet another community. Within two years this latest concrete roadway addition will be sagging under excess capacity. Engineering situations such as this one are repeated annually in most large cities of our country. The only solution to transportation ills in large cities is better mass transit systems and more of them.

This passage is now driven by a specific purpose in a definite direction.

Often, when a writer stumbles and writes falteringly, the reason is either a poorly chosen topic—one that the writer secretly detests or finds boring—or the lack of a clear purpose. These ills cannot be fixed by poring over the syntax of individual sentences or fussing about diction. But they can sometimes be fixed by a re-examination of the writer's purpose.

FIND YOUR POINT

Point and purpose are as closely related as the needle and dial of a compass. The purpose is what you are hoping to achieve, the reaction you want from your reader; the point is your main idea in brief. If you are trying to get your reader to laugh, your point must be funny. If you want your reader to reflect seriously on some grim modern problem, your point must be suitably weighty.

Here is an example of an essay whose point is unclear. The writer thought she began with a straightforward purpose in mind but was unable to crystallize this purpose into an apt point.

```
Fifty years ago jobs were easy to
get straight out of high school, and
```

```
they could be kept until retirement.
World War II had created all of
these jobs because so many factories
were built, and these factories sup-
plied millions of jobs due to mass
production. Today the work environ-
ment has changed. Products made to
order are replacing mass-produced
items. The future appears problemat-
ic. Yet, perhaps all is not hope-
less. Some people believe that a new
middle class is emerging, made up of
workers who know how to maintain
technical equipment.
```

The academic name for the main point of an essay is the *thesis*. Usually this main point or thesis is ritualistically expressed in the final sentence of the opening paragraph—as in this example: "Some people believe that a new middle class is emerging, made up of technicians who know how to maintain technical equipment."

But such a thesis or main point is too wimpy. While she was researching this essay, the writer was delighted by what she saw as new and exciting prospects for women in the technical labor force. Yet, when she wrote the first draft of her opening paragraph, she squashed these opinions for fear that a feministic treatment of the topic would offend her instructor, whom she mistook as a traditional "macho" man.

Indeed, many students believe that in classroom writing they are better off straddling the fence of opinion rather than bluntly taking a stand. We think this attitude is mistaken. Good writing may be moderate in tone, but it is never wishy-washy. Some teachers may discourage the expression of rash opinion unsupported by facts, but precious few prefer timidity to truth. Writing is difficult enough to do well under the best of conditions; it is ten times more difficult if you deliberately muzzle your pen. When it comes to making your point in writing, we recommend the advice of Admiral Farragut as a guiding motto: "Damn the torpedoes! Full speed ahead!"

With encouragement to state what she truly believed, the student rewrote her opening paragraph.

```
Fifty years ago a person could ex-
pect to find a job straight out of
high school and hold that job until
retirement. Women were expected to
stay at home, having babies and
baking pies, while men went off into
```

the corporate jungle to romp with their secretaries and cut big deals. Today all that has changed. Families can no longer afford the luxury of Tarzan venturing out alone into the corporate jungle to forage for the family. Jane now has a new role—as a fellow forager. Today women are likely to be found hacking a career path for themselves in the world of business. Many of these modern women are finding careers in the growing demand for technicians—workers who sit behind computers in factories, laboratories and office towers, monitoring and repairing complex equipment. A new and exciting work force is emerging, consisting of female workers who have learned that they, too, can solve technical problems.

The thesis of this paragraph, as it was in the first paragraph, is conventionally nestled in the arms of its final sentence. But there the similarity between the two paragraphs ends. Before we had oatmeal and gruel; now we have meat and spice. Neither grammar nor syntax can explain this difference. It can only be explained by the writer's newfound willingness to fearlessly express her point.

FIND YOUR POSTURE

"**P**osture" in the conventional sense means the way one stands or poses. One of its synonyms is stance; another is attitude. From the popular discipline of body language, we are taught that posture hints at an inward mood or disposition. Over the years, many of us have learned to read the inner moods of friends, relatives, and even strangers merely from their posture.

A writer's posture similarly signals the mood or disposition the writer holds toward the topic. If you write an essay with a purpose, a point, but no detectable posture, your essay is likely to come out sounding hazy and roundabout, as if you have not quite made up your mind. Here is an example of an essay whose beginning betrays a lack of posture.

```
For many years people have been
attending college. Some people care
more than others about having to be
in school, but to have a good job
they know a college education is
necessary. There are three major
types of college students: students
who care, those who don't, and stu-
dents returning to school after many
years. Each of these students looks
at school from a different perspec-
```

tive. Obviously, not everyone is going to think or feel the same way about one thing.

The writer's main point was to divide students into three rough categories; her purpose was to explain these categories to her reader. But what she communicates in her opening paragraph, and later throughout the body of the essay, is a posture and tone of indifference.

In fact, she was not indifferent. She cared deeply about the topic. She was especially incensed at the uncaring students, regarding them as useless classroom clutter that got in the way of the eager learners. We suggested that she incorporate this posture into her writing. Here is her revised opening.

For many years people have been attending college. Some people care more than others about having to be in school, but to have a good job they know a college education is necessary. There are three major types of college students: students who don't care (they should get out of school and come back later if and when they do care); students returning to school after many years (they should avoid the first group); stu-

dents who do care (they definitely
belong in school).

With the fat shed from the paragraph and the
bone of contention exposed, the writing now
reflects a definite posture.

Well, you say, what if I have not made up my
mind? Our answer is: then you should keep
reading and thinking until you do. To write
expository prose that is crisp and clear requires
a definite posture. The writer must have a
point and a feeling about it, and be willing to
put it down on paper. Read and do the
research necessary to form an opinion before
you begin the writing. Otherwise, an uncertain
posture will cause your prose to waffle. Try
freewriting if you are still unsure about how
you feel. Some writers even work out their
posture as they write. That approach works
for many—including for us—but practicing it

ASSIGNMENT:	Write an essay about a common stereotype in American culture.
TOPIC	The stereotype of the blonde.
PURPOSE	To explain how society views blondes and how blondes view this stereotype.
POINT	The stereotype of the blonde is false and idiotic.
POSTURE	Indignation, anger.

takes uncommon discipline and the willingness to write multiple drafts.

Here is a student essay in which all the invisible elements of purpose, point, and posture come together in opinionated prose. We have listed the elements.

Blondes

Do blondes have more fun? Perhaps, if being stereotyped as bubbly, cheap, and stupid can be considered fun. However, most of the time these accusations and idiotic beliefs are as shallow as the people practicing them.

Any girl who has blonde hair is always and forever bubbling or gushing over something. Right? Wrong. Television has played a major part in this misconception. Series such as "Three's Company," "Charlie's Angels," and "Wheel of Fortune" all feature the classic "dumb blonde." She has big boobs, a dazzling smile, platinum hair, and no brain. This popular misconception of blondes needs correcting. A more realistic spin on the matter is that these are intelligent, mature women who are paid to act. They do not bubble as a way of life, and the only time they giggle is on the way to the bank.

Not only are girls with blonde hair considered giggly, but cheap as well. For some unexplained reason people think blondes are poor, sex-starved beings, lacking either the morals or ambition to say "no" to a man. One example of this belief is found in "Brazen Blonde," an article in *Ms.* magazine, wherein the writer states, "During my teenage years, I dreamed of transforming myself from commonplace brunette to glamorous blonde as soon as I left school. What stopped me was the fear that as a blonde bombshell I could misfire, and instead of being regarded as clever and classy, would be dismissed as dumb and cheap." This example shows how even people who dye their hair are stereotyped as being naturally dumb!

However, being classified as dizzy and cheap is not the only problem blonde girls encounter. People often believe that blonde hair equals brain-dead. I am blonde, naturally, thank you, and I am not stupid. It is very frustrating to have an I.Q. of 150 and to take honors classes

only to hear people mutter "blonde"
under their breath when I don't understand something. Sometimes I even
find myself going along with them
just because it is easier than forever defending myself. I know my attitude is wrong, but it makes things
go more smoothly in relationships
with people. Because of this, I have
come to despise shallow people who
insist on this ridiculous stereotype
being true.

Girls with blonde hair are not the
stupid, ignorant beings they are
made out to be. Often they are
smarter than those who are pointing
fingers at them. If only blonde
people are stupid, then all those
brilliant brunettes should just accept the fact that they are supe-
rior and keep their opinions to
themselves.

To sum up, if your essay is a ship, its destina-
tion is your purpose, its cargo your point, and
the mood of its helmsman your posture. You
may work out purpose, point, and posture
during the actual labor of writing in a process
of tentative discovery requiring much rewriting and many versions of the essay. Or you

may read, think, and make notes until you have a clear enough grip of all three—purpose, point, and posture—to begin the writing. How you work is irrelevant. What matters is that when you begin to write you know your purpose, understand your point, and are certain of your posture.

EXERCISES

❶ For each of the following topics, write down your purpose, point, and posture:

EXAMPLE FOR THE TOPIC "OUR NEWS MEDIA"

PURPOSE   To get the reader to agree that journalists today are wrong in their unbridled pursuit of lurid news.

POINT   When journalists are in hot pursuit of a news item, their excessive investigative fury leads to unfair reportage.

POSTURE   A strong stand against obsessive news reporting.

---

    a. Presidential assassinations
    b. Allowable tax deductions
    c. Labor unions
    d. Criminals and making money off their crimes
    e. Free expression in art

❷ In one or two sentences reveal your posture concerning the following events:

a. The planting of underwater boom boxes to investigate global warming (These boom boxes may destroy the hearing of marine mammals.)

b. Reverse racism on college campuses

c. Universal health care

d. Returning to Russian families properties confiscated by the communists in 1917

❸ Develop a point (thesis) for the following ideas:

a. Forcing corporations to write environmental impact reports

b. The downside of the political correctness movement

c. Having more and more older people in the work force because they refuse to retire at age sixty-five

Make Your Point

Writing is baffling to teach and difficult to learn because there are many different ways to express almost any thought. If this were Freshman Composition heaven, there would be only one word for every concept or object, and for every imaginable thought only one possible sentence. This paragraph, for example, would be written like this because writing it any other way would be impossible.

Unfortunately, we are not in Freshman Composition heaven (nor are we, as faultfinders grumpily claim, in Freshman Composition hell). Instead, we are in some in-between limbo where linguistic freedom makes it possible to express a thought in many different ways. For the English teacher who labors to teach writing on this earthly limbo, the problem is how to condense the principles of good writing from the chaos of individual practice. One way to do this is to teach you how to express your ideas in idealized patterns called *rhetorical modes*.

RHETORICAL MODES

The eight principal rhetorical modes are *narration, description, definition, comparison/contrast*, *division and classification*, *examples*, *causal analysis*, and *process*. These rhetorical modes are idealized forms for organizing your thoughts in an essay. If you learn the ideal form of a comparison/contrast, you can then use this form, if you wish, to compare apples and oranges. If you know how to write a narration, you can adapt the form to tell any story, no matter how homespun or exotic. What you are learning, in effect, are abstract organizing principles that you can apply to any particular essay.

Bear in mind, however, that the rhetorical modes are meant to be handy tools for the writer, not inflexible forms. Indeed, it is the rare essay that practices one rhetorical mode exclusively—that, say, merely describes or compares—and does nothing else. Far more typical is the essay that blends successive paragraphs written in different modes. Nor is it especially uncommon to find a single paragraph that uses a skillful blend of the rhetorical modes to highlight different points. The rhetorical modes, in sum, are meant to help you write an essay, not to dictate sacred form. Writing is a variable and creative act, and no writer should ever feel the cookie-cutter's sense of duty towards any pure form or mold.

Let us say that you have been given this assignment: "Write an essay about an issue existing today between men and women." You think about the subject, narrow it down to the topic of "sexual harassment," and do the necessary reading and research.

Depending on how you work, you could now simply begin to write and hope for a suitable form to emerge from your creative efforts; or you could use one of the eight rhetorical modes as a pre-existing form for your essay. **Narration** For example, you might decide to *narrate* a typical instance of sexual harassment.

```
She was a young black woman with a
nice figure, and when she entered
the office of the professor that
bleak afternoon, she thought she was
applying for a job as his reader. At
first, the professor was genial and
polite, but then she noticed that he
was staring at her body in a way
that made her feel squeamish and
uneasy. His conversation became less
professional and more intimate. He
asked her questions about her
boyfriend, her preference for men,
her sex life. She squirmed and tried
to deflect his attentions without
making him angry. But he was insis-
```

tent. He inched closer to her chair until his knee was touching hers. She froze. The professor was an important figure on campus, widely respected, much published, as well as chairman of her dissertation com-mittee. If she made an enemy of him, she was doomed. She was sitting in the chair, tense and unmoving, when suddenly there was a sharp knock on the door. The professor bolted back-wards in his chair, rolled away from her, and bellowed for the person to enter. She had been saved by a knock.

To narrate is to organize your essay to tell a story. Narration relates details and events in a climactic sequence, focusing on characters and what happens to them. A key element in nar-ration is *pacing,* which means riveting the story only on consequential events while ignoring the insignificant. For example, in the preced-ing paragraph, the writer focuses mainly on the antics of the moonstruck professor. She says nothing about books lining his shelves or the scuffling noises drifting in from the hall-way because these details would have weak-ened the intensity of her focus.

Description Description is first cousin to narration and often walks in its company. Here is how sexual harassment might be written about as a description.

> She sits and squirms in her chair,
> her heart racing, her cheeks flushed
> with shame. Two feet away sits her
> employer, a married man twice her
> age, who has just made an unwanted
> sexual advance at her. He is peering
> up at her eagerly, awaiting an
> answer. A moment ago he hinted that
> if she did what he wanted, she would
> get the promotion she was hoping
> for, and a raise. All she can feel,
> as she sits before him with a hang-
> dog expression, is fear and humilia-
> tion. She wonders what she did to
> provoke his attentions. She is pet-
> rified and ashamed, for all along
> she had thought he was interested in
> her because she was doing a good
> job. Now she is humiliated by the
> truth and does not know what to say.

In writing descriptions, many beginners make the mistake of splattering a shotgun blast of adjectives over the page. But what works better is a laser beam of details that support a *dominant impression*—the most prominent feature of the scene being described. The preceding paragraph, for example, focuses on the fear and humiliation that victims of sexual harassment typically feel.

To describe an object or scene by its dominant feature makes sense, for to do otherwise is to waste time hunting for a peacock among a herd of caribou. The Grand Canyon is a majestic and awesome sight, but no doubt if you searched long and hard enough you could also find in it a smidgen of delicateness—perhaps a tiny bird nesting in the pleat of a rugged cliff. Nevertheless, if you focused your writing at this isolated delicateness and ignored the majestic vistas, your description would be unrepresentative and difficult to support.

Definition Definition is a paragraph or essay organized to explain what a term means. Here is an example.

> Sexual harassment is a term with a definite legal meaning. It is a form of discrimination in employ-ment, prohibited by Title VII of the Federal Civil Rights Act of 1965 and by the Fourteenth Amendment to the United States Constitution. Sexual harassment

applies to employees of either sex.
In order to constitute sexual
harassment, three elements must be
present: 1) offering unwelcome sexual advances, 2) making submission
to these advancements a term or
condition of employment, or 3) having the advancements interfere with
the victim's work and create an
intimidating work environment. Not
all sexual overtures fulfill the
sexual harassment concept. For
instance, two consenting adults
indulging in a sexual tryst does
not constitute sexual harassment.
Sexual harassment means persistent
and unwelcome sexual persecution.

So long as a word is controversial or abstract
enough to provoke argument over its meaning—"love," "patriotism," "self-respect," for
example—it is fair game for a definition essay,
which typically nails down meaning with various strategies. Often it cites the *etymology*
(word history) of the term to show its original
meaning. Frequently, it spends a paragraph or
two saying what the term is *not*—showing, for
example, that sexual harassment is not the
same as an affair. It might even give examples
of sexual harassment. All these paragraphs

share the clarification of meaning as a common aim.

Comparison/Contrast If there is a meat-and-potato dish in the banquet of English composition, it is the comparison/contrast essay, which lists the similarities and differences between two items. Here is sexual harassment treated in this familiar mode.

A clear distinction exists between an affair and sexual harassment. The affair, whether between employees who are either equivalent or subordinate in the pecking order of a company, involves consentual relations between adults. One person is attracted to another, who reciprocates the feeling, and they agree to become romantically involved. The resulting affair may be unprofessional, in bad taste, or against company policy, but it is not sexual harassment. With sexual harassment, on the other hand, the affections and overtures are clearly unwelcomed, usually by the person to whom they are directed. Implicit in them, moreover, is the threat of retaliation if they are not returned. Usually, the two people involved

have an unequal status in the company, with the pursuer being in a
position of authority over the pur-
sued. The presence or absence of
mutual consent clearly distinguishes
the affair from an episode of sexual
harassment. Consent is always present in the affair; it is always
absent in sexual harassment.

The preceding example is a comparison/con-
trast within a single paragraph; longer versions
are waged between paragraphs, with alternat-
ing coverage of the compared/contrasted
items. In a contrast between peas and beans,
for example, one paragraph covers peas,
whereas another successively shows how they
differ from beans. The method you should use
depends on the complexity of your topic. If you
are contrasting two fairly trivial items, say
boxer shorts with briefs, you could probably do
so within paragraphs. On the other hand, if
you were comparing abstract items, such as
self-respect with respect, you might want to
use the wider lens of an interparagraph com-
parison/contrast.

Writing a comparison/contrast is fairly
straightforward: you simply decide on the
bases or yardsticks for your contrast and apply

them systematically to the items being compared or contrasted. For example, if you are comparing love with infatuation, you might decide to use duration, intensity, and outcome as your bases. Your job then is clear: to write about the duration, intensity, and outcome of love as contrasted with the duration, intensity, and outcome of infatuation. Make a list showing love and infatuation matched up side by side against these yardsticks. Transcribe the notes from this list, add transitions, and you have the outline of your essay.

Division and Classification Here is sexual harassment organized as a division/classification.

> Sexual harassment consists of five
> categories of behavior: 1) *quid pro
> quo* requests, 2) sexual slurs, 3)
> offensive sexual conduct, 4) hostile
> or derogatory remarks, and 5) physi-
> cal interference with work. The *quid
> pro quo* category involves a superi-
> or-subordinate relationship in which
> the supervisor or manager demands
> sexual favors in return for employ-
> ment benefits or job advancement.
> The sexual slurs category involves
> hints about a woman's "sexy eyes,"
> "lovely breasts," "seductive walk"

or a man's "firm buttocks" and "sexy physique." It may also involve showing provocative pictures or simply making sexual remarks, such as, "You must be great in bed." Offensive sexual conduct is any conduct the victim finds unwelcome—for instance, kissing, patting, or making obscene gestures. The category of hostile remarks involves comments meant to hurt, such as "God, you're thinking just like a dumb blonde," or "Don't be such a jock," or "Why don't you stick to having babies and cleaning house?" The most serious category is interference with work because it creates a terrifying environment for the victim. Here the harasser forces the victim to kiss, accept an embrace, or to go out on a date by threatening him or her with loss of job if he or she does not comply.

Division and classification means breaking down a whole into its parts. There is a technical difference between dividing and classifying. To sort your classmates into redheads, baldheads, brunettes, and blondes is to divide. To pigeonhole John as a redhead and make assumptions about him because of his hair color is to classify.

Writing division and classification essays sometimes requires exact observations and facts. Other such assignments call for nothing more than imaginative thinking. If you were asked to write an essay dividing literature, you have to know its major types. But if you are to divide and classify your friends, you are expected to be inventive, not exact.

Two errors of thinking rather than of writing commonly bedevil division/classification essays. The first is dividing the whole into incomplete parts; the second is dividing the whole into illogical parts. For example, if you divided literature into its major types and omitted poetry, you would have committed the first blunder. If you wrote an essay dividing your friends into categories, such as intimate, casual, distant, and blonde, you would be guilty of this second lapse because a blonde friend could also be either intimate, casual, or distant. To avoid this error, simply choose one criterion for making your division and stick to it. For example, the criterion behind a division of friends into intimate, casual, and distant is degree of closeness. Stick with that, and your division will naturally reflect a sense of logic.

Examples To write an essay organized by examples is, as the word suggests, to state a point and then give instances that are representative of it. Here is an example applied to sexual harassment.

> Employers or public figures who are accused of sexual harassment may pay a heavy price both in money and bad publicity for their behavior. For example, Robert Packwood, the long-time senator from Oregon, has been under increasing pressure to resign his seat since a number of women, including some of his staffers, have come forward and accused him of sexually harassing them. Another example is the lawsuit filed by Sabino Gutierrez, a male, against his boss, Maria Martinez, who he alleged pressured him for six years to have sex with her under threat of losing his job. In 1993, a Los Angeles jury awarded Gutierrez more than a million dollars in damages. Both examples demonstrate the negative consequences that often result from charges of sexual harassment.

The essay organized around examples is not particularly abstract in structure. It simply states its thesis, and then supports and explains it with either an extended example or a series of pointed examples. In the preceding example, the writer asserts that employers usually pay a heavy price for sexual harassment. Then she proceeds to support that point with two brief examples.

An extended example is a single, comprehensive, and detailed example around which an entire essay is structured. For example, an essay on sexual harassment could easily be structured around the extended example of the infamous "Tailhook" convention at a Las Vegas hotel in September 1991, where twenty-six women—fourteen of them military officers—were forced to run a gauntlet of drunken aviators. Their complaints eventually led to the resignation of the secretary of the navy and of two Navy admirals.

No matter what kind of example you use, be sure that it is truly representative of your point and that you generously use introductory phrases, such as "for example" or "a case in point is," to show where your essay is headed.

Causal Analysis Causal analysis is an essay written either to explain cause or to predict effect. Here's a paragraph on sexual harassment structured as a causal analysis.

    Why is sexual harassment such a hot
    topic today? The answer is compli-

cated but is partly explained by the
numbers. In 1975 there were an esti-
mated 37 million women in the labor
force; by 1990 this number had grown
to over 56 million. By the year 2,005
a projected 71 million women will be
working, nearly half of the antici-
pated labor force. With such large
numbers of women and men thrown together in the workplace, some sexual
harassment is almost bound to occur.
Another explanation is that women
formerly felt reluctant to speak out
because of their fears of economic
retaliation. But with the advent of
feminism, stricter federal and state
laws against sexual harassment, and
with the media exposure given to cel-
ebrated sexual harassment cases such
as Anita Hill's complaints against
Clarence Thomas and the Tailhook convention, women now feel emboldened to
speak out. Because of women's
strengthened position in society,
sexual harassment is treated with im-
mense seriousness in court, and employers have learned to fear the economic consequences of the harasser.

The causal analysis is admittedly an abstract
undertaking. Writing it well depends as much

on your clear thinking as on your writing skills. Frequently, for example, we get essays telling us that violence is caused by insufficient Bible reading; that the acquired immunodeficiency syndrome (AIDS) is an agent of the devil; that sex education in the schools has resulted in the spread of pornography. Some of these arguments, outlandish as they may seem, are often made with a lively persuasiveness. But many of these assertions are personal beliefs rather than provable causes. When you are ready to analyze cause, you should always come to the writing desk well armed with facts and testimonial opinion before you utter even the first allegation.

Causal analysis comes in two parts: either you explain cause, or you predict effect. For example, if you start out by asking why sexual harassment is such a hot topic today, as our sample paragraph does, you are explaining cause. If you analyze the consequences of feminism and attribute to that movement an increased sensitivity to sexual harassment, you are discussing effect. In either case, an essay organized by causal analysis will depend heavily on logic and cited facts.

Process Process, the last of our rhetorical modes, is also regarded as the easiest. An essay organized by process is a how-to accounting of how a procedure should be done or an action taken. Here is a paragraph explaining the steps employers can take to minimize the incidence of sexual harassment.

> The following steps should be taken by employers in an attempt to minimize the possibility of sexual harassment claims: First, prepare an explicit written policy against sexual harassment. Second, clearly and routinely communicate the policy to all employees, explaining the sanctions or punishments involved. Third, express management's strong disapproval of sexual harassment. Fourth, ensure the privacy and safety of individuals who come forward with sexual harassment complaints. Fifth, provide effective remedies and corrective measures for sexual harassment. These steps, if established as policy, will not immunize an employer against sexual harassment incidents, but it will make their occurrence less likely.

The process paragraph or essay is a kin of the cookbook recipe and, because it entails nothing more complicated than an explanation of sequential steps, is usually easy to write. The sad fact is, however, that process writing is frequently muddled, and many manuals meant to explain simple do-it-yourself tasks often leave readers shrieking with frustration. Usually, process explanations break down because the writer assumes a step and does not cover it, or the writer calls a part one name on one page and another name two pages later.

A good rule of thumb is to assume that the reader is entirely uninformed of the process. Explain everything; make sure the steps are sensibly connected and that the writing does not play leapfrog with the logical sequence. Generously lace the writing with pointers, such as "the next stage is . . ." that show the reader where your explanation is headed. The student example paragraph, for instance, uses ordinals to number the steps. Such pointers serve to blaze the trail of the process and steer your reader in the right direction.

USING THE RHETORICAL MODES TO WRITE AN ESSAY

The rhetorical modes are not intended to be ironclad patterns. But using them will allow you to conceptualize a form for your essay in advance of writing it. Some writers can sail out onto the vast ocean of the empty page without the chart of a rhetorical mode and still make a safe landfall. Others find the vastness of the empty page troubling and tend to drift. Whether or not you'll find the modes useful depends on your temperament as a writer. The main point to remember, however, is that the modes are a means to an end, not the end in itself. Your end is to write a solid essay.

The rhetorical modes can help you do that by filtering your topic through a preexisting writing pattern. For example, take an essay assigned on AIDS. Here are possible topics generated by the rhetorical modes:

NARRATION	The story of the discovery of AIDS.
DESCRIPTION	The appearance of an AIDS victim.
DEFINITION	What is AIDS?
COMPARISON/ CONTRAST	The virus that causes AIDS versus an ordinary virus.
DIVISION/ CLASSIFICATION	Progressive stages of the AIDS virus.
EXAMPLES	Examples of prejudice against AIDS victims.
CAUSAL ANALYSIS	What causes AIDS? *Or* The effects of the AIDS virus on a victim's immune system.
PROCESS	Steps you can take to avoid getting the AIDS virus.

Implicit in each topic is the form of a rhetorical mode. To write your essay on any of these narrowed topics, you merely need supporting details and time.

EXERCISES

For each of the following main points (theses), suggest an appropriate strategy of development and give reasons for your choice.

EXAMPLE Loading an Eskimo sled in preparation for a long journey takes hours of planning and work.

STRATEGY Process because the event requires a step-by-step description of how the loading occurs.

❶ When a mother talks to her baby by gurgling, cooing, and gesticulating, some curious responses are evoked.

❷ "Writer's block" is a term that requires careful explanation if it is to be helpful to student writers.

❸ The Oscar-winning motion picture *Schindler's List* depicts with riveting and graphic horror the liquidation of Jews in the Kraków ghetto.

❹ Big-city mayors share many personal characteristics despite their pointedly different management styles.

❺ The grits, greens, chicken, fish, and barbecue sauces of soul food have created a popular boom that reveals different categories of this southern country cooking.

❻ Case studies from the files of social workers in large cities indicate that often eccentrics or social misfits are placed in mental hospitals just because their families want to get rid of them, not because they are mentally ill.

❼ November 3, 1994, was the beginning of the most anguished period of my life so far.

Support Your Point

Good writing is always concrete and specific, never abstract or merely general. It does not linger in the rarefied atmosphere of the anteroom, but, instead, gets down quickly to the grit of the kitchen. If initially abstract, it quickly becomes concrete and specific as in this example.

> *The belief in the existence of monstrous races had endured in the Western world for at least 2,000 years. During that time a rich assortment of semihuman creatures were described by explorers and travelers, whose accounts were largely based on malformed individuals and the desire to enhance their own fame at home. No part of the human body was neglected; each was conceived as having elaborate variations. There were, for example, peoples with tiny heads, with gigantic heads, with pointed heads, with no heads, with detachable heads, with dog heads, with horse heads, with pig snouts and bird beaks. In the absence of knowledge about faraway places (and about the limits of human variation) men populated them with creatures of their imagination.*

> —*Annemarie de Waal Malefijt "Homo Monstrosus"*

The writer opens with a generalization about the popular belief in monstrous races then quickly recounts how such monsters of the day were alleged to look—with misshapen animal heads and bird beaks. Because of these details, we do not have to guess at her meaning.

To write well, you must write specifically. That is what professional writers do. If they begin with a general statement, they quickly get down to the supporting details of facts, observations, and examples. In proportion, these supporting details usually outnumber generalizations in an essay by at least four to one, and sometimes by an even higher ratio. Here is another example, excerpted from a history of the bathtub.

> *The tub itself was of new design and became the grandfather of all the bathtubs of today. Thompson had it made by James Guiness, the leading Cincinnati cabinet maker of those days, and its material was Nicaragua mahogany. It was nearly seven feet long and fully four feet wide. To make it watertight the interior was lined with sheet lead, carefully soldered at the joints. The whole contraption weighed about 1,750 pounds, and the floor of the room in which it was placed had to be reinforced to support it. The exterior was elaborately polished.*

In this luxurious tub Thompson took two baths on December 20, 1842—a cold one at 8 A.M. and a warm one some time during the afternoon. The warm water, heated by the kitchen fire, reached a temperature of 105 degrees. On Christmas day, having a party of gentlemen to dinner, he exhibited the new marvel to them and gave an exhibition of its use, and four of them, including a French visitor, Col. Duchanel, risked plunges into it. The next day all Cincinnati—then a town of about 100,000 people—had heard of it, and the local newspapers described it at length and opened their columns to violent discussions of it.

If you think this is an actual history of the bathtub and find its details fascinating, you are no more duped than the numerous newspaper editors in 1917 who reprinted it as authentic.

In fact, it was a hoax, perpetuated by the American writer H. L. Mencken, who spent a good deal of his professional life twitting people. But what inclines us to believe it even today is its wealth of specific details. We are told not only the day that Thomas took his first bath in the tub but the specific time as well as the temperature of the water. Instead of saying that several other people tried out the bathtub, Mencken invents and names one, the fictitious Col. Duchanel from France.

Mencken's physical description of a bathtub likewise bristles with persuasive specifics. He tells us its dimensions, the way it was made watertight with a lining of lead soldered at the joints, and its exact weight. We are even informed not only that it was made of wood but of Nicaraguan mahagony.

The plain truth about expository prose is this: writing it well does not require a poet's ear, an artist's eye, or a stylist's flair for language. All these traits can help any writing be crisper and better. But nothing can replace supporting details—not imagery, clever phrasing, nor sprightly adjectives. To write expository prose well and convincingly requires you to know your topic well and be able to stack supporting details behind your points. Specifically, you can do the following:

Be Exact Exactness in writing means a preference for the specific over the general, the precise over the approximate. It means naming names, citing dates, giving specifics. In the following example, the writer is an intern relating what he did to prepare for his first surgery:

> The patient was brought into the operating room late that evening. We had waited for him because all the operating rooms in the particular hospital were full. I spent the time before the operation reading a book about surgery and doing surgical exercises. I was, I felt, "ready."

If you are unimpressed with this as a piece of exact writing, your instincts are sound. It is not what the writer wrote, but our doctored version that we have deliberately made fuzzier. Here, instead, is what the writer actually wrote.

> *It was ten o'clock when we wheeled Mr. Polansky to the operating room. At Bellevue, at night, only two operating rooms were kept open—there were six or more going all day—so we had to wait our turn. In the time I had to myself before the operation I had reread the section on appendectomy in the* Atlas of Operative Technique *in our surgical library, and had spent half an hour tying knots on the bedpost in my room. I was, I felt, "ready."*
>
> —William A. Nolan, M.D., "The First Appendectomy,"

Notice the difference: the writer of the second paragraph gives an exact time for the operation, names the patient and the hospital, and tells us not only what book he read but the exercises he did—tying knots around the bedpost.

Invest a similar specificity in your essays, and they will automatically seem better than average. If you say that cigarettes are bad because they give off poisonous gases, name them and describe their harmful effects. If you allege that teenaged drinking is on the increase, look up the numbers and cite them. Digging up such specifics is admittedly not easy, but it is necessary labor in writing expository prose.

Use Descriptive Details Many writers think that vivid descriptions require shrink-wrapping a scene in bolts of colorful similes and metaphors. In fact, sometimes merely saying plainly what you see—enumerating supporting details—is better. Here is an example taken from an eye-witness account of the last moments of a condemned man strapped in the electric chair.

> *The strapped and masked figure sat before us, utterly alone, waiting to be killed. The cap and mask dominated his face. The cap was nothing more than a sponge encased in a leather shell with a metal piece at the top to accent the electrode. It looked decrepit and resembled a cheap, ill-fitting toupee. The mask, made entirely of leather, appeared soiled and worn. It had two parts. The*

> *bottom part covered the chin and the mouth, the top the eyes and the lower forehead. Only the nose was exposed. The effect of the rigidly restrained body, together with the bizarre cap and the protruding nose, was nothing short of grotesque. A faceless man breathed before us in a tragicomic trance, waiting for a blast of electricity that would extinguish his life. Endless seconds passed. His last act was to swallow, nervously, pathetically, with his Adam's apple bobbing. I was struck by that simple movement then, and can't forget it even now. It told me, as nothing else did, that in the prisoner's restrained body, behind that mask, lurked a fellow human being who, at some level, however primitive, knew or sensed himself to be moments from death.*
>
> — Robert Johnson, *"This Man Has Expired"*

The writer rivets his description on the appearance of the condemned man, recording in minutiae everything about him from the mask and the cap he is forced to wear to the bobbing of his Adam's apple. This is what you must do if you wish to write well: zoom in on the scene and pile on the specifics.

Cite Facts   A fact is an accurate representation of reality and the one piece of detail you can include that is most likely to sway your reader.

Facts must be diligently dug up out of library books or mined from the brains of experts. Either way, getting the facts is rarely easy. But facts add such an authoritative edge to prose that including them is definitely worth the digging. Here is an example.

At the turn of this century, infectious diseases were the primary health menace to this nation. Acute respiratory conditions such as pneumonia and influenza were the major killers. Tuberculosis, too, drained the nation's vitality. Gastrointestinal infections decimated the child population. A great era of environmental control helped change all this. Water and milk supplies were made safe. Engineers constructed systems to handle and treat perilous wastes and to render them safe. Food sanitation and personal hygiene became a way of life. Continual labors of public health workers diminished death rates of mothers and their infants. Countless children were vaccinated. Tuberculosis was brought under control. True, new environmental hazards replaced the old. But people survived to suffer them. In 1900, the average person in the United States rarely eked out fifty years of life. Some twenty years have since been added to this life expectancy.

—*Benjamin A. Kogan,* Health: Man in a Changing Environment

These representations are facts and their accuracy easily verified. It is easy to imagine how vague and mushy this could have sounded had we not been told specific facts about pneumonia and influenza, changes in the sanitary engineering, and the increase in life expectancy.

Quote Statistics   The statistic is a fact clad in a numerical overcoat. Citing statistics without benumbing the reader takes a deft touch. Here is an example from a book about the sorry plight of single men in society.

> *Excluding the divorced and widowed, there are a little over 4,000,000 single men between 25 and 75. About 7 percent are inmates in correctional or mental institutions. This leaves about 3,650,000 on the loose. Of these, about 330,000 are unemployed or unregistered in the labor force, leaving 3,320,000 single men at work. They do not tend to work very hard, however. Only a little more than 60 percent were on the job full time—a little higher than single women, about 20 percent behind married men.*
>
>   *In general, the 3,320,000 single male workers hardly earned enough to feed themselves and buy Playboy magazine, let alone follow its philosophy. In 1970, their average*

income was approximately $6000, their median income $5800.

— *George Gilder,* The Naked Nomads: Unmarried Men in America

Too many numbers will drive even a hardened government statistician over the brink. But a tablespoon of statistics sprinkled here and there over a paragraph or two will make your writing sound briskly authoritative.

Beware, however, of biased or skewed statistics. Numbers are causeless mercenaries that can be recruited to fight on any side. For instance, because a campus poll on a study-abroad program will be answered mainly by those interested in the issue, the resulting statistic may not accurately reflect the views of the entire student body. To say that "Four out of five doctors recommend Themogenics 2000 as a diet complement" is meaningless until you know how many doctors were polled. If only five were, the statistic is fluff. Moreover, persuasive statistics are always up to date. A paper on, say, sexual harassment should therefore not quote statistics from past decades when harassment was rarely reported.

Cite Authority and Testimonial Opinion   The world is an arena where all opinion is not respected equally. If you are a famous man or woman, if you have made a name for yourself as an expert, your opinion counts more than the opinion of the average man or woman. That is the reason why writers so often cite authority opinion. To do so is simply to say, "See! So and so, a famous man or woman, agrees with me on this point." Here is an example.

> *You express a great deal of anxiety over our willingness to break laws. This is certainly a legitimate concern. Since we so diligently urge people to obey the Supreme Court's decision of 1954 outlawing segregation in the public schools, at first glance it may seem rather paradoxical for us consciously to break laws. One may well ask: "How can you advocate breaking some laws and obeying others?" The answer lies in the fact that there are two kinds of laws: just and unjust. I would be the first to advocate obeying just laws. One has not only a legal but a moral responsibility to obey just laws. Conversely, one has a moral responsibility to disobey unjust laws. I would agree with St. Augustine that "an unjust law is no law at all."*
>
> —*Martin Luther King, Jr., "Letter from a Birmingham Jail"*

Dr. King is advocating a revolutionary line of thought for an ordinary citizen and a dissenter, as he was thought to be at the time, but invoking the authority of a saint who agrees with him greatly supports his case. Now that Dr. King is himself a famous man, he is often quoted as an authority on moral issues, much as he once quoted Saint Augustine.

When you quote the famous, remember that not all the famous are equally famous. Some enjoy such towering fame—St. Augustine, for example, Socrates, Plato, and Dr. King himself—that merely naming them is sufficient introduction before quoting their opinion. Other experts are not famous enough to require no introduction. In such cases, you merely write, "As Dr. Jane Brown, an astrophysicist at Podunk University, put it...." And then you quote what the doctor said.

Sometimes the quoted person is no authority, simply one who has "been there" and, because of experience, can contribute testimonial opinion to the discussion. In the following example, the writer quotes longtime residents of the West to describe living in wide open spaces:

To live and work in this kind of open country, with its hundred mile views, is to lose the distinction between background and foreground. When I asked an older ranch hand to describe

Wyoming's openness, he said, "It's all a bunch of nothing—wind and rattlesnakes—and so much of it you can't tell where you're going or where you've been and it don't make much difference." John, a sheepman I know, is tall and handsome and has an explosive temperament. He has a perfect intuition about people and sheep. They call him "Highpockets," because he's so long-legged; his graceful stride matches the distances he has to cover. He says, "Open space hasn't affected me at all. It's all the people moving in on it." The huge ranch he was born on takes up much of one county and spreads into another state; to put 100,000 miles on his pickup in three years and never leave home is not unusual. A friend of mine has an aunt who ranched on Powder River and didn't go off her place for eleven years. When her husband died, she quickly moved to town, bought a car, and drove around the States to see what she'd been missing.

— Gretel Ehrlich, *"Wyoming: The Solace of Open Spaces"*

The writer tells us little about John, the "older ranch hand," and the friend's aunt, other than to state that they live in the West and therefore have the knowledge about its "wide open spaces."

Establishing the credentials of a witness is all you really need to do when introducing testimony. Remember, however, that expertise in one field does not necessarily transfer to another. For example, the world-famous clothing designer, Ives Saint Laurent, would make a strong witness on the merchandising of women's apparel. But his opinions on earthquake preparedness do not carry a similar authority.

Use Reason Issues of faith or belief can seldom be resolved by the enumeration of hard facts or statistics. You cannot, for example, convince a sincere believer to disavow God by citing facts. Nor can you prove with facts that an act, such as, say, abortion, is immoral if someone fervently believes otherwise. But sometimes the best supporting detail is a reasoned argument, where appeals are made to logic, custom, or common sense. Here is an example of solid reasoning used to support a point about crime.

> *If crime were really the result of willful depravity, we should be ready to concede that capital punishment may serve as a deterrent to the criminally inclined. But it is hardly probable that the great majority of people refrain from killing their neighbors because they are afraid; they refrain because they have never had the inclination. Human beings are creatures of*

habit; and, as a rule, they are not in the habit of
killing. The circumstances that lead to killings
are manifold, but in a particular individual the
inducing cause is not easily found. In one case,
homicide may have been induced by indigestion
in the killer. In another, it may be traceable to
some weakness inherited from a remote ances-
tor; but that it results from something *tangible*
and understandable, if all the facts were known,
must be plain to everyone who believes in cause
and effect.

—*Clarence Darrow, "The Futility of the Death Penalty"*

Reasoning such as this may be the best way
available to you in support of a point that
hinges on faith or belief. If you have no facts
behind your point, you must at least have logic.

The reasoning you cite should reflect the
qualities of objectivity, common sense, and
fairness. To be objective is to remain detached
on an issue, and to try to sort out the facts from
popular opinion and prejudice. History teaches many lessons about the fallibility of popular
belief. Scurvy, for example, was once thought
to be a disease of shirkers and punished by
flogging until James Lind showed in 1750 that
it came from a vitamin C deficiency. Many
topical issues are similarly confused by parti-

san emotions. The debate about the health care system is a classic example, with advocates of either side charging the other with paternalism, greed, or socialism. To separate fact from such emotion requires a cool, objective head.

Common sense is another ally the thinker must use to combat the paranoid theories with which every generation has had its credulity assailed. In the 1960s, for example, it was rumored that major bankers were conspiring to take over governing the world. Among some quarters, this ridiculous hearsay was actually taken seriously. Today it seems only laughable. Yet we also have our share of crackpot beliefs presently in circulation. For instance, in 1993 a published report accused the government of spreading the AIDS virus to control the population. Another charged that the milk supply had been laced with leukemia. Such unrestrained claims fly in the face of common sense. Why should the government be spreading AIDS while spending millions of dollars in research to fight it? Generations of children have thrived on milk, so why believe the leukemia conspiracy theory? The world has enough real hardship in it already and needs no bogus woes. Use your common sense when faced with an outlandish claim or rumor.

If you are objective and exercise common sense, chances are you will also be fair. To be fair is to be willing to hear out the other side of an argument. Many multisided issues bedevil us today. Arguments rage concerning the death penalty, animal experiments, illegal aliens, and passive smoking. To be fair is also to put little stock in the plague of common stereotypes about people. Women are stereotyped as emotional rather than logical; Jews as greedy financiers; police as brutal racists; and Italians as passionate lovers. To avoid stereotyping, remind yourself that people and institutions seldom fit into neat categories, and that critical thinking requires you to judge each on individual merit.

Give Examples   The example is a kind of fact. You may give either long or short examples in illustration and support of your points (see Chapter 4, pp. 65–67). Here is a paragraph that cites short examples.

> *The evils of word availability have been impressed on us ever since the women's liberation movement first drew attention to them at the beginning of the 1970s. Language consecrates the subordinate role of women in the loss of surnames at marriage, in the labeling of wed*

or unwed status by Mrs. *and* Miss *(marital-status labeling is not required of men), in the greater caution expected of women in speech (women are more "polite" than men), in the many opprobrious names for women (*slut, gossip, crone, hoyden, slattern—*the list is endless), in the contempt attached to* spinster *but not to* bachelor, *and in hosts of other ways. Even an epithet for males is an indirect slap at the female:* son of a bitch. *The network of associations among these verbal habits traps us in a set of attitudes from which we can extricate ourselves only by earnest attention to both the attitude and the words.*

—*David Bolinger, "Mind in the Grip of Language"*

But sometimes you are better off supporting your point with an extended example, demonstrated in this excerpt.

Even the shrewdest of men cannot always judge what is useful and what is not. There never was a man so ingeniously practical in judging the useful as Thomas Alva Edison, surely the greatest inventor who ever lived, and we can take him as our example.

In 1868, he patented his first invention. It was a device to record votes mechanically. By using it, congressmen could press a button and all their votes would be instantly recorded and totaled. There was no question but that the invention worked; it remained only to sell it. A congressman whom Edison consulted, however, told him, with mingled amusement and horror, that there wasn't a chance of the invention's being accepted, however unfailingly it might work.

A slow vote, it seemed, was sometimes a political necessity. Some congressmen might have their opinions changed in the course of a slow vote where a quick vote might, in a moment of emotion, commit Congress to something undesirable.

Edison, chagrined, learned his lesson. After that, he decided never to invent anything unless he was sure it was needed and wanted and not merely because it worked.

—*Isaac Asimov, "Of What Use?"*

This example nicely supports the point that "Even the shrewdest of men cannot always judge what is useful and what is not."

The lesson of this chapter is simple: be specific in your writing. If your essay contains too many generalities, it will seem vague and perplexing. In the following example, the student had a point to make about the commitment in marriage. But she merely repeats the same generalization and without adding anything concrete to clarify her meaning.

> Marriage is a close and intimate union that a man and a woman decide to make after falling in love. It is a difficult commitment to make. Marriage is for life and is total commitment to one another. Men and women today tend to forget the commitment they have made to their spouses. They sometimes violate this sacred commitment by the act of having sexual intercourse with someone other than the lawful spouse, which is wrong and unforgivable.

What she says, even if true, is unconvincing. Without specifics, we do not know what she means by commitment, why it is difficult, and what act or acts would make it total.

What kinds of specifics? Her peer writing group came up with a list. They felt that she needed to supply details of what one spouse must do to show commitment to the other. Must the husband surrender his paycheck at the end of the week? Must the wife also become a breadwinner to take the financial burden off the husband?

Must they alternate cooking dinner? Exactly what does showing "commitment" entail?

Here is how the student revised the paragraph.

    Marriage is a close and intimate union that a man and a woman decide to make after falling in love. It is a difficult commitment to make. For the man, commitment means he must be faithful and true to her, that he must give up his nights out with the boys, that he must be loyal to her when she is down, and that when she is cranky because it is her time of the month, he must be understanding. For the woman, it means that she must stand by him through thick and thin, try to understand him when he is moody and feels trapped in a dead-end job, nurse him through sickness, and pump up his ego when his boss or some trivial incident of the day has deflated it. For both, commitment means giving up sexual relations with any other but the lawful spouse for the mutual good of the marriage.

The second paragraph is more specific and better communicates what the writer means by "commitment." It is also a sprightlier paragraph with a livelier trot partly because it is not so weighted down by gummy generalizations.

Contrary to what you may think, writing does not begin with the act of jotting down words on the page or typing on the computer keyboard. It begins much earlier, in the thinking you do about the topic, in the digging you do to unearth supporting details. To avoid overly general writing, do your homework. Do not begin the writing, especially if your assignment is an objective one, until you have the facts. Burrow into the library sources and interview experts so that when you finally sit down to write, the supporting details you need will be at your fingertips.

EXERCISES

❶ Find two descriptive details to support each of the following points:

EXAMPLE

POINT.
In California state officials cared enough about the gorgeous Garibaldi fish to stop hunters from spearing them.

FIRST DETAIL.
Named after an Italian general who wore garish tunics, the bright orange Garibaldi is a flamboyant sight that attracts hundreds of underwater photographers and fish hunters each year.

SECOND DETAIL.
Recently these spectacular fish have been showing up in private aquariums, where they are prized as decorative items resembling the poppy, the monarch butterfly, or brightly plumed birds.

---

a. *Point.* Our global population needs to be curbed despite the fact that some people feel squeamish about directing people's reproductive lives.

b. *Point.* Talk shows have become a platform for exposing the worst side of human behavior.

❷ Quote an appropriate authority for each of the following points:

EXAMPLE

POINT.   School funding should be based on a consumption tax, not a property tax.

QUOTATION. Joel Fox, a columnist for the *Los Angeles Times*, suggests that "Historically, property taxes were a levy on productive land. Those who worked the land gave part of their bounty to the feudal lord protecting them. Today, in most states, residents are taxed on an arbitrary value of the property. . . . As home values increase and earning power remains flat, the onerous aspects of the property tax become obvious."

a. *Point.* The Victorian Age, so often seen as a time of certainty and definite social mores, was in actuality a time of religious uncertainty and social revolution.

b. *Point.* Researchers from the Institute of Human Origins at University of California at Berkeley and Tel Aviv University in Israel believe they have discovered the first nearly complete skull of the oldest-known ancestor of humans.

❸ Use an example or illustration to support each of the following points:

EXAMPLE

POINT. The $250 billion national information infrastructure plan, supported by the White House, will produce a data highway whose economic and educational benefits will be far-reaching.

ILLUSTRATION. For instance, school rooms will be wired to have access to movies, newspapers, and television programs all over the world and will be able to transmit information to the same areas. Users will be able to post information for all to see and will be able to hunt for specific information stored in global computers.

a. *Point.* The growing number of students who possess guns is bound to contribute to the growing number of violent incidents on campuses.

b. *Point.* In the 1990s, while England's Tory Party was legislating a program of family values, scandal after scandal erupted within its ranks.

Clarify Your Point

A chapter on clarifying your point is essentially a chapter on style. And style of writing, like style of dress, varies both with the writer and the times. Not so many years ago the fashionable style was to write in long, rolling sentences whose clauses rumbled or curled across the page. Today we prefer a lean style altogether trimmed of wordiness. Such changes in style evolve mainly through magazines and newspapers whose writing the public is fed daily. For example, consider this description of the last moments of the English poet Tennyson, which appeared in a nineteenth-century magazine.

> *Then the stars came out and looked in at the big mullioned window, and those within them saw them grow brighter and brighter, until at last a moon—a harvest moon for splendour, though it was an October moon—sailed slowly up and flooded the room with golden light. The bed on which Lord Tennyson lay, now very near to the gate of death, and with his left hand still resting on his Shakespeare, was in deep darkness; the rest of the room lit up with the glory of the*

night, which poured in through the uncurtained windows. And thus, without pain, without a struggle, the greatest of England's poets passed away.

— *Frank Harris, "My Life and Loves,"* Pall Mall Gazette.

Ouch! a modern editor would choke before mercilessly chopping this passage off at the root.

What traits do we value today in a modern writing style? The answer, especially with expository writing, is clarity.

Clarity in writing means penning sentences that read as we expect them to, that do not startle us with any sudden shifts, and that do not baffle with an indigestible vocabulary. It is prose that seems natural and effortless, allowing us to absorb what the writer has to say without being confused by any eccentricities of style.

Writing such prose is never easy. It takes effort and time. It requires a willingness to rewrite your sentences until your meaning is crisp and clear. Often, it commits the writer to a tedious number of drafts. Although there are many elements to clarity as well as various prescriptions for achieving it, our own view is that clarity presupposes at least three ingredients: plainness, brevity, and variety.

PLAINNESS

Plain prose is prose dressed in an everyday business suit instead of a gaudy costume. It does not draw attention to itself, but says what it means without straining for effect. Its opposite is pretentious prose, as in this example.

> The leitmotiv of current anthropology study is to isolate the subject in the environment in which it demonstrates its uninhibited characteristics. Such laboratory-like isolation relieves the harried researcher from the Heisenbergian dilemma of artificially influencing the particular object under scrutiny by the scholastic and academic act of studying it.

What is this all about? When we asked we discovered that the underlying thought the writer was laboring to express was simply this:

> Today in anthropology the trend is to study subjects in their natural environment. Doing so minimizes the possibility of researchers' artificially influencing the subject being studied.

Later, the writer admitted that because her topic was anthropology, she had tried to sound scientific. To her, sounding scientific meant sounding self-important. Many scientific articles do, indeed, exude an air of self-importance, but the best are clearly written.

To write plainly, you must write in your own down-to-earth voice—the one you might use with someone older whom you respect, whose opinion you value, but before whom you do not feel completely cowed. This person could be, say, a favorite uncle or aunt or anyone of kindly authority. If that person should ask you how you are, you would be inclined to say, "I am well"—not, "I am functioning at a level of optimal wellness."

To write plainly is also to write in predictable sentences. All good sentences conform to an expected pattern. We hear the beginning of a sentence and anticipate a certain ending. But if the sentence suddenly departs from its expected pattern, it is likely to confuse us. Consider this example.

```
In this phase of the occupation
focuses on the cruelty heaped on the
villagers.
```

A simple correction makes it clearer.

```
In this phase of the occupation the
focus is on the cruelty heaped on
the villagers.
```

                    or

```
This phase of the occupation focuses
on the cruelty heaped on the vil-
lagers.
```

Here is another sentence whose pattern is similarly muddled.

```
For most children—their minds curi-
ous, their personalities exuberant,
and fears being well defined—fairy
tales are an influential source of
knowledge.
```

With two repetitive structures beginning with "their" and a third abruptly abandoning the pattern, the sentence is confusing. Read this improved version.

```
For most children—their minds curi-
ous, their personalities exuberant,
and their fears well defined—fairy
tales are an influential source of
knowledge.
```

The rewrite makes all three phrases parallel and completes the expected pattern of the sentence. The following examples demonstrate the importance of plainness:

Not plain:

```
The reign of Catherine the Great was
tyrannical and marked by decrees,
lacking in mercy, and also filled
with scandalous love intrigues.
```

Plain:

```
The reign of Catherine the Great was
marked by tyrannical decrees, merci-
lessness, and scandalous love
intrigues.
```

Use the Active Voice Writing plainly will require you to write as much as possible in the active voice. The active voice is a verb form that identifies who has done what in the sentence. In the sentence, "Jan punched John in the mouth," we know what happened and who did it. The passive equivalent, "John was punched in the mouth," hides who did the punching.

Because it hides accountability, the passive voice has become the henchman of committee reports. Consider this sentence: "The full cost of the program was withheld from the finance committee." But by whom? The active voice blabs the truth: "Dean Milliken withheld the full cost of the program from the finance committee." Here is another example: "It was decided to raise the fee on student parking." The same sentence in the active voice names the guilty: "The Student Affairs Committee decided to raise the fee on student parking."

With the exception of government babble, most everyday writing uses the active voice, as it should. The one usage that justifies the passive voice is when what was done to the subject is more important than who did it. For example, in this sentence, "The innocent civilians were slaughtered [by the drunken soldiers]," the passive justly spotlights the horror done to the civilians. Or, "The test procedures were carefully monitored over a period of six years." This particular sentence, from a scientific paper, uses the passive voice to emphasize the objectivity of the monitoring. Who did the monitoring is unimportant.

Write in Speech Rhythms Because we talk more than we either write or read, the rhythms of speech have become more familiar to us than the formal constructions of writing. If you wish to write plainly, you should try to write in these rhythms, especially of polite speech. Here are examples of sentences where the rhythms strike us as more bookish than oral.

> *To predict that any poet who uses adjectives to excess and active verbs too little is destined to develop a depressive psychosis would be an exaggerated claim.*

Here is how this sentence might be written in a more speech-like rhythm.

> *We would exaggerate if we said that a poet who uses too many adjectives and too few verbs was likely to go mad with depression.*

Some written sentences are so utterly creatures of the page that, read aloud, they flop around furiously in the mouth. Here is one such, from the same book that the preceding was taken.

> *If we add to a passive, withdrawn diction the disjunctive, incoherent syntax and both of these to a poetic content expressing fear and anxiety as well as an inadequacy of affect, it is possible to outline a constellation of effects which, taken together, suggest depressive psychosis as that form of mental disturbance most likely to develop.*

A good rule of thumb for judging the orality of your sentences is the one-breath gauge. If the sentence cannot be read in one breath by a healthy person, it does not resemble speech.

BREVITY

Brevity in writing means using as few words as necessary. Because the universal law of writing dictates that initial drafts are usually longer than necessary, to achieve brevity typically means cutting your text. Some writing teachers even recommend discarding all first pages. This we think a little drastic—after all, sometimes a first page may turn out flawless.

Nevertheless, the theory behind that advice is sound. When we write, we start out searching for what we mean to say, and typically find our opinion and voice only by the second or third page. First drafts, therefore, always begin badly; second drafts are usually better but still flawed; it is only the third and fourth drafts that are fit to be seen in public.

Many strategies exist for achieving brevity, but behind them all is the principle of repeated rewriting. As you rewrite, you should try to do the following:

- Prune deadwood
- Avoid redundancies
- Choose first-degree words

Prune Deadwood Some familiar word clumps serve as a needless filler in our speech and writing. Among such clumps are "despite the fact that," "in the event that," "it is incumbent on," "after all is said and done," "by leaps and bounds," "last but by no means least," "regardless of the fact that," and "in this modern world of today."

For the sake of brevity—to say nothing of clarity—get in the habit of thinning these clots of words. "Despite the fact that Napoleon won the Battle of Austerlitz, he did not conquer Russia" can become "Although Napoleon won the Battle of Austerlitz, he did not conquer Russia." "In the event that the U.S. wins a gold Olympic medal in cross-country skiing, I shall be amazed" can be shortened to "If the U.S. wins a gold Olympic medal in cross-country skiing, I shall be amazed." "It is incumbent on us" is more plainly stated as "We must." "After all is said and done" really means "Clearly." "Last but by no means least" is just a fatty version of "Last." "Regardless of the fact that" can become "although."

Cutting deadwood is not easy to do and requires difficult choices. Sometimes you must deliberately dump some wonderful image or phrase along with the brackish brew in which it floats. In the following paragraph we have bracketed words that can be deleted without harm to the text:

```
[The disease of] Bronchitis is
[quite clearly] an inflammation of
the membrane lining the [air pas-
sages or] bronchial tubes of the
lungs and causes [the] narrowing of
these air passages. Irritation of
```

mucus-producing glands within the mucus membrane results in [the production of] excess bronchial secretions. The main symptoms of bronchitis are coughing and [increased expectoration of sputum, better known as] spitting up phlegm. The condition may also produce wheezing and shortness of breath [intake]. In severe cases, the patient may look blue [in color] and have a bloated [look in his] face. Bronchitis may be [of] either [an] acute [type] or chronic [type].

Another source of deadwood is the phrase "in the area of." It is difficult to think of an instance in which a simple "in" cannot replace this bushy phrase. In the following example, taken from the newsletter of a professional psychic society, the writer is describing the potential importance of certain research.

In the area of health, the coupling of traditional medical cures in the use of mind-initiated cures could be advanced. In the area of investigative work, "emotional imprints" have been used by skilled sensitives to trace past events in archaeological and police investigations. In the area of education, the ability of the human mind to

> obtain information at various levels has been indicated as an important factor in successful decision making by executives. In the area of national defense, there are the obvious implications of one's ability to project to distant sites and affect sensitive instruments or other humans.

Here is the same passage with "in the area of" transformed into "in":

> In health, the coupling of traditional medical cures in the use of mind-initiated cures could be advanced. In investigative work, "emotional imprints" have been used by skilled sensitives to trace past events in archaeological and police investigations. In education, the ability of the human mind to obtain information at various levels has been indicated as an important factor in successful decision making by executives. In national defense, there are the obvious implications of one's ability to project to distant sites and affect sensitive instruments or other humans.

You should likewise snip off those cousins of "in the area of" whose names are "in terms of" or "in the field of" and replace them with "in." Similarly, "in order to" can usually become "to" without loss of effect or meaning. For example, the sentence "We went shopping downtown in order to save money," becomes, "To save money, we went shopping downtown," or "We went shopping downtown to save money."

Avoid Redundancies   Redundancies are duplicate words that can be cut. What is the point in writing, "The students gave a full and complete report of the cheating incident" when "full" and "complete" have the same meaning? "The students gave a full report of the cheating incident" is enough. Certain common redundant pairs are fair game for amputation: "in this day and age" should be cut to "today." "Most important and foremost," should become either "most important" or "foremost." "For all intents and purposes" can be written as "actually." Here are other redundancies, followed by shorter versions:

REDUNDANT	The average person of the Renaissance period never questioned the miracles of Jesus.
BRIEF	The average person of the Renaissance never questioned the miracles of Jesus.
REDUNDANT	The canvas was large in size and square in shape.
BRIEF	The canvas was large and square.
REDUNDANT	In his role as an accused Irish bomb setter, Daniel Day Lewis was made up to look like a hoodlum in appearance.
BRIEF	In his role as an accused Irish bomb setter, Daniel Day Lewis was made up to look like a hoodlum.
REDUNDANT	Today the cadaverous and thin look is stylish.
BRIEF	Today the cadaverous look is stylish.

Some redundancies are caused by a multiadjective pileup of synonyms before a noun. Here is an example.

> **REDUNDANT** He writes in an orotund, florid, ornamental, embellishing style.

For ourselves, we think one apt adjective, or at the most two, should be equal to the task of describing any noun.

> **BRIEF** He writes in a florid style.

Choose First-Degree Words   Words are roughly lumped into two categories: first- and second-degree words. First-degree words immediately suggest an underlying image, object, action, or concept. Second-degree words are more complex synonyms one step removed from the original meaning. "Lie" is a first-degree word, "prevaricate" its second-degree synonym. The meaning of "lie" we all learned in the rough and tumble of childhood. "Billy don't lie to me!" a parent would scold just before defining "lie" with a swat. Few of us, however, have ever been swatted because we "prevaricated." We probably stumbled over that salon word in a book and learned from a dictionary that it means "to lie."

Whenever possible, you should use first-degree words for their heightened immediacy. Here is a list of some second-degree words followed by their first-degree equivalents:

Second-Degree Word	First-Degree Word
Habitation	Home
Terminate	End
Deprivation	Loss
Substitute	Replace
Benisons	Blessings
Unintelligent	Stupid

To get an example of the enormous difference first-degree words can make to writing, consider these two paragraphs. The first uses only second-degree words; the second uses their first-degree equivalents.

The natural *habitation* of the beaver is a wetland or pond in the woods. The *deprivation* of this animal's *habitation* can mean the *termination* of the beaver and, eventually, of humans. No strip-mall can *substitute* for the *benisons* of wildlife and woodlands. If we do not care about this *deprivation*, we are *unintelligent.*

The natural *home* of the beaver is a wetland or pond in the woods. The

loss of this animal's *home* can mean
the *end* of the beaver and, eventually, of humans. No strip-mall can
replace the *blessings* of wildlife
and woodlands. If we do not care
about this *loss,* we are *stupid.*

The striking difference between these passages
is argument enough for using first-degree
words.

Note that it is a mistake to think the shorter
word is always more understandable than a
longer one. Usually, that's the case but not
always. For example, consider this sentence,
taken from an acclaimed manual of style.

> *There are occasions when obscurity serves a lit-
> erary yearning, if not a literary purpose, and
> there are writers whose* mien *is more overcast
> than clear.*

> —*Wiliam Strunk, Jr., and E. B. White,
> "The Elements of Style, 3/E"*

Mien is a short word but not commonly
known; its synonyms—"appearance" and
"mannerisms"—although longer, are more
likely to be familiar to readers.

Our own instinct is to use the word that
strikes as the most accurate for the particular
context. In revising, if we judge our first
choice as either too stuffy, stilted, or difficult,

we replace it with a simpler equivalent. Faced with an absolute choice between accuracy and understandability, we opt for accuracy, even if doing so means driving the reader to the dictionary.

VARIETY

Many beginning writers, especially when grappling with an unfamiliar topic, tend to write in monotonous rhythms, their sentences uncoiling in the same repetitive patterns. Your ear must help you to cultivate a varied rhythm to your writing, but a good first step is never to begin several sentences in a row with the same word and phrasing. Here is an example.

```
A jealous husband is afraid to lose
the one he loves. A jealous husband
is a suspicious person. A jealous
husband asks many questions and is
never satisfied with the answers.
```

With a little tinkering, we can add a pulse of variety into this passage.

```
A jealous husband is suspicious and
afraid to lose the one he loves.
Because of his suspicions, he asks
many questions and is never satis-
fied with the answers.
```

One way to achieve variety in your writing is through sentence combining. For example, consider these three basic sentences:

- It is a portrait.
- It is less a portrait of a man.
- It is more a portrait of a way of life.

Notice how easily the three can be combined into one.

```
It is a portrait but less of a man
than of a way of life.
```

The revised version is leaner and more effective. Here is another group.

- I saw my father's stooping figure.
- He was wearing his familiar straw hat.
- He was almost completely hidden by his beloved rose bushes.
- It was the last view I ever had of this hardy Idaho dairy farmer.

Now here is the combination.

```
The stooping figure of my father,
almost hidden by his beloved rose
bushes and wearing his familiar
straw hat, was the last view I had
of this hardy Idaho dairy farmer.
```

Like everything else, sentence combining improves with practice.

Use Figurative Language Figurative language —an apt simile or metaphor—can flash the illumination of a lightning bolt over a hazy sentence. Unfortunately, no one can teach you a formula for writing a sparkling image. That must spring from your own imagination. Nevertheless, if you can think of an apt image, by all means use it to energize your writing. Here is an example.

In the community of living tissues, the uncontrolled mob of misfits that is cancer behaves like a gang of perpetually wilding adolescents. They are juvenile delinquents of cellular society.

Likening cancer to an unruly mob of juvenile delinquents gives a vivid explanation of the deadly disease.

Writing with crisp details, next to writing with imagery, is the second best means of adding color to your text. Here is an example from William Manchester's biography of Winston Churchill.

Sometimes, as Cecily ("Chips") Gemmell will recall, the opening hour is "ghastly." There is no diverting him. A stenographer peers through a window and observes blithely: "It's dark out-side." Churchill, giving her a bleak look, replies pitilessly: "It generally is at night." His creative flow is blocked; he will prowl around, fling himself into a chair, bury his head in his hands and mutter, "Christ, I've got to do this speech, and I can't do it, I CAN'T." On such occasions, Inspector Thompson notes, Winston is "a kicker of wastebaskets, with an unbelievably ungovernable bundle of bad temper. It is better to stay away from him at such times, and this his family seeks to do."

If you can think of no sparkling image to add to your prose, use crisp details and the effect on your writing will be every bit as vivid. But if your choice is between no image and a stale one, choose none and make your point in straightforward language. Trite imagery adds nothing. Here are examples of trite figures of speech.

- ▸ Flat as a pancake
- ▸ High as a kite
- ▸ Swallowed the canary
- ▸ White as a ghost (or a sheet)
- ▸ Burn the candle at both ends
- ▸ Have your cake and eat it too
- ▸ In broad daylight

- Fast as lightning
- Straight as an arrow
- Spending an arm and a leg
- Sleep like a log
- Nip the problem in the bud

Another trap with using imagery is the mixed metaphor, whose contribution to prose is often unintended buffoonery. Here is a mixed metaphor that smears mud on a star:

    His lucky star blossomed out of the
    soil of his poverty.

Plainness is better here:

    His luck grew out of his poverty.

Here are a few more examples of mixed metaphors, followed by corrections:

NO: Associating with her is playing with fire and could get him in deep water.

YES: Associating with her is dangerous; he could be badly hurt.

NO: The wheel of fortune turns, proving that life is a seesaw.

YES: Life is fickle with many ups and downs.

Writing clearly means writing innumerable drafts, going repeatedly over your text, cutting, adding, and transposing. You must tackle your prose successively with an ax, a scalpel, and sandpaper because the process of revision involves big initial cuts and then progressively smaller ones as the final draft emerges. If the writing pours effortlessly onto the page, it is probably unclear. As the English playwright Richard Sheridan said, "Easy writing's vile hard reading." The opposite of this proposition—that difficult writing makes easy reading —is also a universal truth.

EXERCISES

❶ Recast the following sentences to make them plainer and more like your own speech:

> a. By all concurrence of signs, as scientific men solemnly study the calculated change in position of the earth, a detrimental earthquake could occur.
>
> b. His mordant humor truncated his friends' affections.
>
> c. Her uncle bequeathed her a significantly large financial legacy.
>
> d. To come into acquisition of the knowledge requisite to being a good public orator is a lifelong and cumulative task.

❷ Change the following sentences from passive to active voice (supply an actor if needed):

    a. Extreme political views are held by these Mafia types.

    b. Her long and crooked nose was changed into a straight, cute snubnose.

    c. The Senate expects that a consensus-building chief justice will be appointed by the president.

    d. The architectural plans for the mission were stolen.

❸ In the following sentences, strike out each word that does not add significantly to the meaning of the sentence, paying special attention to redundancies:

    a. Within one hour's time, this decisive decision could scuttle, abort, and sink the most important deal in years.

    b. A person who has been an important influence in my life so far is most certainly the woman who gave me birth, my mother.

    c. As a youth, he did not have many choices or options because he grew up in a bad neighborhood, riddled with violence and poverty.

    d. The field of mathematics and the area of genetic research are still looking for brilliant minds that can figure things out.

    e. He is tall in stature; his hair is red in color; and his eyes are piercingly blue as well as large in size.

❹ Combine each of the following sentence clusters into one clear sentence:

EXAMPLE

All is in readiness.

The funeral director calls a staff conference.

There is a reason for the staff conference.

It is to make sure that each assistant knows his precise duties.

The combined sentence follows:

When all is in readiness, the funeral director calls a staff conference to make sure that each assistant knows his precise duties.

    a. Bilingual education has provided needed leverage.

This leverage is visible at all levels of the educational system.

It has moved districts away from cultural deficit approaches.

Minorities have labored and suffered for so long in these approaches.

    b. I was reading.

A shadow crossed my page.

I saw a golden female moth flap into the fire and get fried in seconds.

She was big and had a two-inch wing span.

c. According to Phyllis Schlafly, it was not the strident demands of the women's liberationists that brought high prizes to women's tennis.
Actually it was an important discovery by sports promoters.
They discovered that beautiful female legs gracefully moving around the court made women's tennis highly marketable.
It was marketable because it delighted male audiences.

d. She had loved her father too.
She loved him in a different way.
She depended on him and felt secure with him.
At the age of fifty-four he married again.

Index